DREAM
WHISPERS

Carolynn McCully

BALBOA.
PRESS

A DIVISION OF HAY HOUSE

Balboa Press books may be ordered through booksellers or by contacting:

Balboa Press
A Division of Hay House
1663 Liberty Drive
Bloomington, IN 47403
www.balboapress.com
1 (877) 407-4847

Because of the dynamic nature of the Internet, any web addresses or
links contained in this book may have changed since publication and
may no longer be valid. The views expressed in this work are solely those
of the author and do not necessarily reflect the views of the publisher,
and the publisher hereby disclaims any responsibility for them.

The author of this book does not dispense medical advice or prescribe
the use of any technique as a form of treatment for physical, emotional,
or medical problems without the advice of a physician, either directly
or indirectly. The intent of the author is only to offer information
of a general nature to help you in your quest for emotional and
spiritual well-being. In the event you use any of the information in
this book for yourself, which is your constitutional right, the author
and the publisher assume no responsibility for your actions.

Any people depicted in stock imagery provided by Thinkstock are
models, and such images are being used for illustrative purposes only.
Certain stock imagery © Thinkstock.

Print information available on the last page.

ISBN: 978-1-5043-5292-5 (sc)
ISBN: 978-1-5043-5293-2 (e)

Balboa Press rev. date: 05/25/2016

I dedicate this book with heartfelt appreciation
to my beloved sisters, Suzanne and Gail, who
continue to inspire me with love and appreciation
for the world of nature. I thank them for their
encouragement to put my unusual experience with
life energy awareness to paper. As a sister and guest,
I am forever grateful for all the magical moments
spent in their loving, warm hospitality and for being
connected to such wonderful travelling companions.

Special thanks go out to my friend Glenys and my daughter Ellen. Both have been a tremendous help with editing suggestions, insightful ideas, and influencing necessary changes. I am especially appreciative for my daughter's ongoing support and understanding for a work in progress with the intention of becoming a delightful, enchanting read.

CONTENTS

INTRODUCTION

A mind that is stretched by a new
experience can never go back to its old
dimensions.

Oliver Wendell Holmes, Jr.

The human desire to connect with nature unquestionably
provides for fascinating learning along with any wisdom
gained from a sought-after experience. Perhaps nature
also desires a similar connection, offering unique
life awareness possibilities to what occurs in a shared
journey. No matter the source of connection, the
desire to express one's learning would most assuredly
be enjoyable to those willing to listen.

Cedrina, a little red cedar bench, unveils growing
awareness throughout her adventurous life journey.
Memory flashes from her past persist through
awakening dream whispers longing to be heard.
Cedrina's story comes to you as a whimsical tale filled
with charming life reflections, unusual connections,
and energy-sharing opportunities. These enlightening

experiences take place in a small alcove entrance of a rural country home far from the forest and lake surroundings of her past-life energy existence as a maturing red cedar tree.

'*Your deepest roots are in nature. No matter who you are, where you live, or what kind of life you lead, you remain irrevocably linked with the rest of creation.*'

Charles Cook

ENCHANTMENT
BEGINS

---•◆•---

WATER'S EDGE GIFT

The motivation underpinning Cedrina's story begins with an eagerly accepted invitation to camp out at a lake property nestled high in the mountains of British Columbia. This visit will provide the opportunity to share and enjoy a world of nature, where life and tranquillity intertwine in breathtaking beauty. It was the kind of rest and relaxation required (at least for this particular guest) that could only be found in such a harmonious setting. Camping in the middle of such a delightful forest area would turn out to be a most inspiring ending to a lovely but hectic summer vacation. Getting back to nature was the perfect means to bringing calmness to heart and mind before embarking on the long journey home. The excited guest could not help but feel tremendous appreciation for the opportunity to unwind in such a charm-filled atmosphere.

Settling into this enchanting environment began with a quick trek into the surrounding campsite area that would allow a firsthand glimpse of nature's appeal, whetting the appetite for all that could be expected in the days ahead. It took but a moment for the peace and serenity of this alluring setting to soak in. The quick tour offered a tempting impression of having stepped into a small corner of the Garden of Eden. The visiting guest, so thoroughly impressed with this first taste of quiet charm, eagerly awaited to become further lost in enchantment. It was the first time that such an in-depth enticement to connect with nature had taken such a strong hold on the heart and mind of the captivated guest.

Majestic mountains were the backdrop of a breathtaking view of the peaceful lake where the campsite was located. A thorough exploration of the lake and surrounding area was high on the list of things to do over the next few sunshine-filled days. By being so fully immersed in the sights and sounds of nature, one could not help but become spellbound with tantalizing notions of imaginative forest life and story possibilities. During this visit, a warm midday turned out to be the perfect time for a stroll to the beachfront. While enjoying the slight cooling breeze coming off the lake, the guest's attention was drawn to a strange-looking object resting in the pebbles at the water's edge. Filled with a fascination at the marvel of nature so easily available, she felt it only natural to follow her intuitive urge to investigate. At first glance it appeared to be a small piece of driftwood.

Intrigued by the driftwood's unusual shape, small size, and dull-gray coating, the guest eagerly picked up what she first thought was a lifeless piece of wood, and she momentarily held it close to her heart. After turning it over in her hands, she brushed off loose bits of dirt and sand. Her heart momentarily quickened with awareness when she began to feel a most peculiar faint vibration coming from within the driftwood. The astonishing moment left a distinct impression. *This is much more than an old piece of dead wood.* She was captivated by a passing thought. *Perhaps all life forms really do hold some kind of undying energy, even this old, weathered piece of driftwood.* It was this unexpected notion that immediately became the inspirational tone of what was to follow. Without a moment's hesitation, the guest decided that this little gift from the lake would become a special keepsake, a reminder of her most intriguing connection with nature's enchanting energy.

On her return to the campsite, the little piece of driftwood was placed on a large rock along with a collection of smaller stones she had gathered during the day's outing. For the rest of the day, the guest pondered the increasing sense of mystery and intrigue that this piece of wood had evoked. A strange awakening to magical thinking triggered her curiosity to the hidden secrets of nature's energy yet to be discovered. Her curiosity and imagination were indeed running free and wild during what turned out to be an extraordinary and delightful day.

As the day progressed, she decided that such an inspirational gift deserved a thorough cleanup that only her tender care could provide. *And who can tell,* she mused. *Perhaps this little driftwood treasure has an important and insightful message to share.* Even its shape and position, as it rested gracefully on the rocks with extending root tentacles, reminded her of something sacred. Its outstretched arms, seemingly clasped in a posture of prayer, begged to be noticed. The posture alone gave her the impression this piece of wood had something important to declare. All that was necessary was for someone to take the time to listen. It was impossible to resist such a plea for attention. While entertaining these fanciful ideas and thoughts, the guest began experiencing a strange and simultaneously old and familiar feeling. A new door of discovery slowly opened before her.

Later in the evening, before heading down to the campfire, she gathered the necessary tools for a decisive cleaning procedure to ready the piece for the next step, a vital and vigorous sanding. Great care would be needed to dig out the debris that had collected over time in the driftwood crevices. The guest was astonished with the depth of hopeful anticipation she felt with the amount of attention required to bring this little piece of driftwood back to life. It felt like she was about to embark on what could only be described as a quest of nature's energy, in order to uncover the mysteries of this unique little piece of wood. As she settled in at the fire-pit with sandpaper and a sharp knife close at hand, she was finally ready to begin a new and disarming energy discovery journey.

Incredibly, the guest found that once she picked the driftwood up off the nearby rock, she again experienced the tingling sensation. It was identical to the faint vibration she'd felt earlier at the water's edge during that first moment of contact. Her curiosity soared as she brought the little piece of driftwood up to her ear. *'What is it you have to say to me?'* She was astonished with an unexpected response to her query. She actually heard a faint whisper, like a distant but clear echo. *Open the door to heart and mind. Explore and enjoy each of life's moments.* She shook her head in amazement, unsure of what it meant. It was at this point that she began to doubt her own reality-based thinking, and she ultimately decided to turn her attention to the cleaning task at hand.

The origin of this beguiling piece of old wood was revealed as she smoothed away the rough gray outer shell. A warm, rich colour slowly emerged with her firm but gentle sanding. This new discovery both surprised and delighted her. This unearthing prodded further attentiveness and a determination to continue in spite of the intense energy and incessant sanding required. Soon, her efforts paid off in the revelation of a breathtaking display of symmetrical graining, with streaks of pink and red throughout the curves of the wood. The guest was delighted to discover that her little driftwood treasure was undoubtedly a small root portion of a red cedar. After she finished sanding, she buffed the piece and gently set it aside on the picnic table for the night. Turning towards her sleeping quarters to retire, she let out a deep, sigh of contentment. The guest smiled inwardly and thought to herself, *I wonder who actually discovered whom?*

While preparing for bed after the exhausting day of trekking through the forest and strolling by the lake, the guest reflected on the connection that took place with the little piece of wood. This remarkable, vibrational experience could only be viewed as incredible. *If a lifeless object like this piece of driftwood is capable of whispering through this sort of vibrational energy,* she thought, *can it also communicate with other life- forms as well? Is such a thing even possible?* Turning out the lights and shutting her eyes in the hopes of slowing her racing thoughts was the first of many attempts to get a good night's sleep, but it was especially difficult when unfettered imagination was in full swing. She realized sleep would remain elusive and just out of reach. Nevertheless, the magical connections with nature's energy experienced that day, paved the way for dream whispers filled with nature's mystical life-form connections all through the night.

In spite of little sleep and an early rise, the guest felt fresh and strangely euphoric as she headed down to the fire-pit to welcome the morning sunrise. It was a mystifying and joy-filled occasion. As she arrived at the picnic table, the guest was greeted by a most surprising spectacle: the very first rays of the morning sun gently stroked the little piece of driftwood, intensifying the richness of newly exposed red cedar graining. For one thrilling moment, a surreal glow radiated from the extraordinary treasure. The sight triggered an untold appreciation for the energy force of nature. A door of awareness had definitely opened to her, and through it a new path of appreciation for all life-form connections awaited. She thought to herself, *perhaps through this little gift from the lake, an opportunity would arise as a means to fulfil the growing inspiration she felt to share her exceptional experience.* It did not take long before her unusual creative thinking took over, providing possibilities in a story form to explore and share nature's energy experience with others. This unique nature connection took root deep in the heart and mind of this author, that very guest.

Moment of Reflection

When one is totally absorbed in such an extraordinary occurrence, the experience reaffirms and inspires reflective thinking about life-force energy in all of creation.

'Open the door to heart and mind … Explore and enjoy each life moment.' On that magical day, an intriguing door opened for me. It expanded my heart and filled my mind with a desire to express a portion of my life learning through a tale based on the exploration of this driftwood experience.

This is my story.

CEDRINA
AWAKENS

THE LITTLE ALCOVE

The awakening season had arrived, and it brought with it the gifts of spring energy and light with the promise of warmer days ahead. Facing east, the rural country home was in a perfect position to capture that first magical glow of early dawn. If one listened carefully, sweet sounds of engagement could be heard with echoes of chirping and chattering taking place throughout the trees. Numerous small flying creatures beckoned the arrival of a new day. The large picture window provided a clear view of the winged ones, cloaked in magnificent flashes of colour, flitting from tree to tree. Spring had truly arrived.

Any moment now, the sun's rays would begin a predictable journey, rising up over the far horizon, sending its magical light across the fields, and then slowly crossing the lawn to its final destination. The little alcove was awakened just as the light shone through the front entrance window, bringing morning delight to all in its path. As if it was to be expected, with each early spring, the very first rays streaming through the window provided the small room with a brilliant spectacle of beams. A delightful awakening from early sunrise energy would soon replace the deep sleep of winter. It was a most stimulating wake-up call for Cedrina, the little red cedar bench lost in a deep winter's fog.

The cedar bench was set against a plain wall in the little alcove hallway and offset with an oversized mirror carefully positioned just above the cosy seating area. This sitting arrangement, made up solely of the little red cedar storage chest that doubled as a comfortable bench turned out to be a pleasurable place to relax to enjoy a delightful view of the great outdoors. Although large for the size of the room, the mirror contributed greatly to the illusion of greater space, especially with the effects from reflected light rays. This small alcove area was now filled with the magnificent brilliance of early daylight.

Standing guard in the corner of the room, in close proximity to the bench, was a tall, shiny black hat rack looking totally out of character in such a cosy, inviting space. The rack seemed to emit a cool indifference, giving one the impression of unresponsive life energy stemming from an out-of-place, high-gloss appearance. The rigid hat rack was in complete contrast to the vibrant, warm energy coming from the natural wood glow of the red cedar bench. One would wonder why such an inharmonious oddity was placed there in the first place – other than, of course, being a convenient place to hang hats. In spite of everything, the tall rack's close proximity did provide a smidgen of comfort to

Cedrina as a constant reminder of a most interesting time of life from her distant past.

Already shrouded in mystery, the rack was even more puzzling by the barely noticeable markings found around the block base. Although hardly detectable, one could still make out vague indented lines through the heavy layers of paint. Strangely enough, the markings shared a slight resemblance with the easy-to-distinguish Latin words found on the backrest of the little bench. *'Heri Foveat – Cras Somnnia – Vivere Hodie,' was* carefully carved, and the words' meaning and reason for being placed there, at least at the present time, were just as baffling as the Latin name of Cedrina, given to the bench. Perhaps the desires for answers to this puzzling mystery would one day come to fruition.

At this time of year, Cedrina was often haunted and yet thrilled with pleasant but fading memories that arrived each spring. These lingering dream-like memories portrayed the little bench as a cedar tree surrounded by forest trees standing tall and straight, reaching high into the clouds. In one of these dreams, there was an abundance of smaller trees among dense foliage that overshadowed a young sapling found trembling and filled with apprehension within the crowded surroundings. Cedrina, dismayed by this dream and fully aware of the vulnerability that encompassed the tiny sapling, became cloaked in an aura of great strength. This strength came from the fading recollection that she too once stood tall and straight with strong, healthy, outstretched branches thick with sweet-smelling leaf foliage collecting life energy from warm rays of the great light. Could this be a deep core feeling of expansion that happened at this time of year? It was, after all, the season where the sudden burst of light into the alcove space created a pathway to easily slip in and out of a dream-memory world of the past.

It was within these early spring arousals, while being lulled into a semblance of contentment from her unique memories as a forest tree, that Cedrina was filled with pride in the knowledge that many life- forms found nourishment and shelter within her once thick, fragrant branches. The little bench thoroughly enjoyed pondering on her delightful recollections, even if they were only a product of imagination found in dream form. No matter – it was more important to hold on to the fleeting pleasures received from what was turning out to be fast-fading recollections. Cedrina's dream-memories were becoming harder to discern as real, without the daily contact of a natural forest environment to keep them alive. She began to see them more as dream whispers, sometimes overflowing with delightful awareness tales of life energy connections, but always filled with intrigue and adventure. She found it strange that her dreams seemed to be most prevalent during a tree's natural growing season.

Focusing on the alcove brought Cedrina into awareness that warm, mid-morning daylight had replaced the earlier awakening rays. It was such a welcoming space to reconnect with all of life, especially the lovely homeowners whom Cedrina called her 'Dear Ones,' and who would be arriving soon to share in the cosy alcove. These dear humans evoked a unique connection with nature, evidenced in the love and care extended to home and surrounding property. It was as if they held a deep-seeded agreement to care for and appreciate what could only be shared between the available human and nature relationship. These dear humans viewed all of nature as being filled with great beauty and profound service – and most assuredly deserving of all the kindness and consideration a human could provide in the exchange. The presence of these dear humans brought assurance to Cedrina's ongoing pleasure-filled desire of connection to human energy.

Like clockwork, as part of a mid-morning custom, the Dear Ones would quietly enter the space and set themselves gently on the soft, comfortable cushion atop the little cedar bench. Once settled, they then took a moment or two to gaze out the front window and appreciate the great outdoors before planning their day. This unique couple found it a perfect backdrop for their morning routine of quiet solitude, basking in the wonderful energy of light as they soaked in the welcoming, warm rays of early spring.

Soon to join the peace and solitude would be a small, four-legged, furry creature aptly named by the bench as Furry Four Legs. Upon entering, the furry creature would begin a captivating morning ritual of attachment to the Dear Ones. Before settling in, the usual action of Furry Four Legs was to rhythmically knead and dig its claws into the padded covering on top of the smooth, sweet-smelling cedar bench. A demonstration of affection and greeting to the humans to whom it had become so attached was easily detected by the most intriguing sound of purring. This distinctive sound filled the atmosphere, growing in volume and vibrancy as the furry creature achieved the intended energy connection goal. During this special morning ritual, the Dear Ones quietly sat, leisurely sipping from cups of intriguing liquid that emitted a pleasurable, rich aroma, adding to the cosiness of the pleasant alcove scene.

PERSISTENCE AND FREEDOM

During this particular morning, Furry Four Legs was distracted by a very tiny flying creature's frantic movements as it attempted to escape to the great outdoors. This hopeless quest to freedom was made up of continued attempts flying towards the outdoor light, only to be blocked by the clear glass window barrier keeping it captive. Although trapped and unable to succeed with an intention of escape, the tiny creature was deserving of credit for perseverance. What Cedrina observed was a relentless exhibition of determination and undying persistence to achieve a freedom that would only be found in the great outdoors. Unfortunately, this freedom escape plan, seemingly so close to the tiny creature, was in reality doomed for failure. Success could be possible, if only the tiny one did not lack the necessary powers to fly through glass. It seemed that this particular creature would meet its demise in the confines of the alcove after all.

Suddenly in one fluid motion, a flying ball of fur leaped off the bench and into the air. With a lightning-swift paw movement; Furry Four Legs captured the winged creature, landing softly on the floor. Thankfully it was only a moment before the tiny one, so close to meeting its demise in the jaws of a voracious ball of fur, received an instant reprieve. The tiny one managed to evade an ill fate by escaping to safety when the furry paw was lifted to investigate the captured prize. In the blink of a cat's eye, it flew straight up and away, safely avoiding recapture. At least for the present, flying a bit higher, its determination for a successful getaway was renewed.

It was the jumping jack antics of Furry Four Legs that soon broke the previous daydreaming spell that had filled the atmosphere of the alcove. The bouncing about created such a disturbance to the peace and tranquillity of the moment, and awareness of the winged creature's plight slowly seeped into the consciousness of the Dear Ones. The past moment of reverie was now replaced by giggling pleasure while watching the amusing actions of their tiny, furry pet. Regrettably, at least for Cedrina, it was a lost opportunity for connection, sabotaged by the impetus actions of Furry Four Legs and the winged creature's quickly depleting energy. The previous vibrant energy of the tiny creature was now at such a low frequency that the required energy to connect and share in life awareness was no longer achievable.

A flight path had emerged between the mirror and window, with a periodic stop to recover on top of one of the hats resting so precariously in the arms the hat rack. This journey's path would prove quite the challenge to the little flying creature, which was avoiding the quick swats from Furry Four Legs, but it was still the only hope in the frantic search for an opening to the great outdoors. The hypnotic and repetitious movement was finally broken in a moment of compassion, when one of the Dear Ones intervened. The tiny creature was rescued from a doomed outcome. Loving hands provided the exhausted creature a stay of execution as the front door quickly swung open for a quick release. This very kind gesture would allow a fresh burst of energy and a shortcut in the winged creature's flight to freedom. Escape to the great outdoors at last! The peaceful tranquillity in the little alcove, allowing for quiet reflection, was once again established.

Renewed hope for Cedrina slowly emerged while observing the precarious position of the winged creature's drama. The final outcome of freedom provided reassurance that, in spite of odds to the contrary, dreams and intentions really can come true. By holding steadfast to the intent of escape and simply not giving up, a successful ending was the final result, at least for the little winged creature. Interesting that in this particular case, a literal door of freedom was opened, revealing a chance of new life adventure. Cedrina concluded this intriguing act of compassion as an example to the energy of love in action.

For the next while, Cedrina would find herself immersed in a dream world of slowly opening doors. Each door opening filled with hopeful opportunities of sharing connection with other life energies, replacing a growing awareness to the futility of her failed tree destiny. Dreams of red cedar energy providing service to others would remain alive a little longer. One never knows – perhaps for Cedrina too, a door would actually open, allowing her the freedom to express her life story. Such an opening would bring her peace and contentment to replace the slow-building uneasiness presently being experienced.

Oddly enough, once the Dear Ones left the alcove, there was a momentary flash of memory to a time and place far in the past as a young cedar, filled with a strange sensation of tiny creatures digging into her outer bark with intention to reach and devour bits of soft wood matter. Strong, vibrational sensations and the sounds of buzzing seemed to accompany this memory, leaving Cedrina yet again wondering if it were real or imagined.

Moment of Reflection

Hopes, dreams, and desire — all seem to hold a significant energy force that brings power to inevitable outcomes.

Could it be that outcomes are determined by observable action, drawing others into the desires and thus strengthening the possibility of success?

Of course, self-sabotaging energy works by the same principle only with misdirected emotional energy from what is desired tied closely to the deeper sense of what is deserved or not.

Perhaps the life-force energy found in all life forms is subject to some type of ability to draw strength from others in order to meet intended desires or needs?

CLOUD OF UNCERTAINTY

Another new day beckons. Cedrina is awakened from deep sleep by the soothing household energy of the Dear Ones. This energy is made up of rich aromas and sounds of morning meal preparation. A leisurely awakening accompanied by the morning's early light became the threshold for the fading memory-dreams of her past to emerge. This time, however, awareness of a growing melancholy ever so slowly gained a firm grip. This emerging sensation was triggered by a brief recollection moment that involved a looming threat of being smothered by creeping tentacles of an invasive, fast-growing vine capable of blocking the great light's rays. This particular vine sometimes took root and grew among the forest floor foliage that had surrounded a little cedar sapling so long ago. Cedrina, now in bench form, was once more reminded that no longer would her branches reach out to welcome the great light as it once did.

The quickly fading dream-memories of Cedrina as a young tree were replaced by a vibration of dulling energy. This diminishing awareness was expanding and growing in strength. Little by little, a space of hollowness was building within her core. Adding to the intensity of this ebbing sensation, the household atmosphere seemed to be in a state of chaos, indicating something unusual was taking place. The resulting confusion only added to Cedrina's expanding discomfort to what was gradually becoming a fear of an unknown future.

A dream-memory of a thick, dark cloud growing and expanding in density and power, little by little, took over the once cloudless blue sky began to surface. The growing darkness brings with it a dreary foreboding of a colossal storm of destruction, ready to descend. This memory left Cedrina in a state of disquiet, recalling raging storms of the past that had created a great deal of havoc. In spite of being protected by the forest, there was an element of helplessness that diminished one's energy happening outside of one's control. Perhaps this helpless, fear-based sensation was the natural order of aging. Cedrina wondered if the Dear Ones, whose life energy was aging much faster, felt the same way.

Having to adjust to yet another transitional change, with no sign of fulfilling a desire to find an outlet to express her past and present learning, was turning into a disturbing reality for the little bench. What would the next stage bring? After all, her Dear Ones would one day move on to a new life adventure. These musings brought back a conversation between the dear humans in the alcove while taking in their early morning solitude. The little bench had become aware that a huge transition was soon to take place in the form of a complete household move. Would the Dear Ones retain their contact to the little bench no matter where they go?

Pondering this move proved perplexing for the little bench. Over time the Dear Ones had gathered many belongings, some of which were precious hand crafted items. Due to this upcoming move and having to make huge lifestyle changes, the Dear Ones were caught in a dilemma, deciding which possessions would have to be sold or passed on to others. This new awareness brought an increase of apprehension regarding the future for Cedrina. Yet from somewhere deep within, Cedrina remained unruffled with the profound understanding that energy connections continually come and go during one's life-time and eventually all become only dream memories. Unless a miraculous connection soon occurred, her shared journey with the dear humans would also fade into a mysterious cloud, dissipating into the atmosphere of oblivion.

Cedrina kept mulling over possibilities of finding a receptor to listen to her unique story over the passing growth seasons. Not having an outlet was all the more wearisome when considering that in the forest environment of the past, tales of experiences and life purpose were fully understood and easily passed on within the natural surroundings. It was well understood, in her tree life state, that insight from important knowledge accumulated each season would automatically be passed on to new seedlings and the surrounding younger trees through awareness connections. However, the simplicity of relating life stories in her present circumstances, as that of a bench far out of reach from the nature-filled environment of the past, turned out to be an unexpected challenge faced by the little red cedar.

This frustrating circumstance intensified Cedrina's desire to connect to a human who could absorb and understand significant information that had grown over time. It seemed to Cedrina that with the outpouring of vibrational energy she was recently sensing, time was quickly running out for even more unique core energy experiences that were bursting at the seams to be told. Oddly enough, the transformation to her present form could also be considered her particular cedar tree-life fulfilment, having lived with the very deep desire to connect and be of service to humans. And so at this critical time, Cedrina was filled with doubt and dread for the future, and she was quite sensitive to the coming of yet another significant change.

Being trapped in this cycle of disappointment over reaching a tree's natural destiny would repeatedly haunt the little bench over the next while. Cedrina continued to question herself about how to truly fulfil her past destiny during this time of vibrational ebbing. Was it even possible to return to the natural state within the surroundings of loving Mother Earth? It was quite the dilemma for Cedrina. In spite of receiving enjoyment with her human connection, she still retained remnants of life energy as a young cedar tree filled with predestined desires. Waves of uncertainty surrounding her natural sense of cedar purpose continued. There must be something more, a piece of information that was missing, that would bring solace to the hollowness growing within her cedar core.

Cedrina hoped that eventually this growing discomfort and insecurity about her future would pass, and that the present day circumstances would somehow turn once again to one of contentment. Although it seemed a lost cause, there was always the prospect of a significant human connection sprouting up. She tried to remain optimistic, and her focus was turned to the arrival of early spring and new life, bringing with it sweet and fresh energy – albeit much too slowly for Cedrina.

Cedrina, caught up in a confusing, back-and-forth duel of appreciation and disappointment, likened this upheaval awareness to a howling wind storm that blows swift and strong, slows to a breeze, and then picks up again, threatening all that is not deeply rooted and secured in a sanctuary. Adding to this sparing confusion, a miniscule sensation of relief crept into awareness, much like a distant approaching fog, emerging in the forest. It came as a surreal intuitive dream that was just out of reach. It seemed to Cedrina that this veiled dream was also filled with appreciation for all the life expression opportunities that came in both her life-form states and untold unique energy connections. Cedrina could only hope that as the days progressed, so too would the slowly approaching fog lift, bringing relief from the back-and-forth teetering turmoil that was presently taking place.

Moment of Reflection

It's strange how the same experiences that bring wisdom and knowledge can become a bone of contention without the means to express what has been learned.

In the later stages of life, frustration and disillusionment often leave one wondering, 'What was this life experience really all about? Is it really even necessary to leave any of one's journey and life-learning behind?'

Perhaps simply experiencing life is enough.

This yearning to tell one's story does trigger one to question, 'Who and what am I really all about? If there really is a life-purpose, what is it?'

ALCOVE ADJUSTMENT

A different type of energy awareness seeped through as a slow, penetrating whisper to the little bench. Soon a visiting house guest would be arriving to stay for a time, throughout the moving transition period. New and exciting household energy ran rampant as the Dear Ones prepared for this new arrival. Preparation of food and activities were discussed in the early morning visits to the alcove. The usual peace and calm were replaced by excitement and anticipation that electrified the little room. The humans were elated that this special loved one would be helping in preparation for all the changes that were soon to take place. They had received an acceptance phone call that indicated she felt compelled to come after having experienced such a strong, heartfelt urge to assist.

So many questions arose as Cedrina contemplated possible outcomes from this visitor's arrival. Would the Dear Ones' guest join them in their mid-morning ritual, and would this guest also find it a peaceful retreat? After all, everyone in the household knew and understood that there was no better spot to experience such an abundance of joy and contentment to the awakening of a new day. Curiosity took hold as Cedrina pondered. Would this temporary household addition be receptive as a life awareness connection? Perhaps the fog of uncertainty was finally lifting. Cedrina could not hold back a renewed hopefulness that was fast overcoming the uneasiness of the past little while. It was a tremendous relief when nagging doubt began to dissipate, replaced by an unstoppable delight of optimism and expectation as the arrival time quickly descended on the happy household.

Caught up in anticipation of the great changes about to take place, a renewed attempt at connection was made with the unapproachable hat rack. Perhaps with this new, high energy flowing through the household, a different outcome from all the other attempts at connection could actually take place. This of course was not her first try, and as usual, an impenetrable aura seemed to engulf the hat rack, revealing little familiar life-form energy to Cedrina. Not to be deterred, the little bench could not give up or give in to the futility of it all. If truth be told, at least at this point, weariness was beginning to creep in with a lack of response to her connection attempts. For reasons unknown to Cedrina, there remained a minuscule spark of elusive energy from the hat rack trying desperately to seep through, but, seemingly blocked in some manner. This alone kept Cedrina hopeful, because it was like being aware of a muffled whisper, just not quite clear enough to discern. Could it be due to the rack's appearance and impassable outer layers of cold, dark thick paint? Perplexing as it was, there remained a nagging curiosity and instinctive questioning to life-energy beginnings of this cool, aloof hat rack.

Somewhere in the core of the little bench, there lived a spark of familiarity beckoning Cedrina not to give up, although these efforts left little joy to be shared. And so it continued, day after day. Cedrina would reach out to the hat rack, extending a willingness to connect by sending out an energy message relating, *'I am aware of you, so tall and unyielding with your connection energy … And yet, your presence reminds me of a place I once belonged.'* After the first statement, she gave a short pause, waiting in the hope for a response. The statement would be followed by a deeper acknowledgement. *'I realize you are unable to share deep core wisdom, although I sense there is something deep within, hidden behind all those covering layers bursting to be expressed.'* With frustration slowly building, Cedrina carefully continued. *'In spite of this failure to connect, a mere courteous response would be most appreciated.'* Another moment of eager anticipation before disappointment again sets in. Deafening silence hung heavy as a barrier between them. The cool rejection lingered on for a moment or two in the little alcove's atmosphere. *Ah well,* mused Cedrina, remembering the persistence of the tiny winged creature a few mornings past. *It was worth a try!*

Setting aside this dreary outcome, Cedrina reflected on a memory of a chilly winter's day some time ago. It was the day that the hat rack first arrived to the little alcove space. Cedrina considered it as a most peculiar day, recalling having flashes of energy that awakened her from the lull of a deep winter's sleep. If this whispered memory served her correctly, there was eager anticipation accompanied by spurts of unbounded joy during the few hope-filled moments with the rack's entry to the little alcove space.

Previous to that day, there was only the mirror for company. In spite of no story-sharing opportunities because the core energy of the mirror did not originate from a natural wood source, pleasure was still possible with the delightful, reflective light show that took place each first light. Cedrina felt it a privilege to be placed underneath such a splendid object, and if truth be told, she was pleased with the opportunity of pretence, adding energy and balance to the magical illusion of space provided by the mirror.

To the Dear Ones, the mirror offered a firsthand view to the comings and goings through the front door, as well as an excellent vantage point reflecting the passing of seasons. During seasonal changes, many dream memories would trickle through to Cedrina, keeping hope alive for the day when that very door would open, giving way to a true and clearer picture of her elusive tree life past. Ah, yes – there was much to be desired and appreciated regarding alcove position. Cedrina pondered on the stimulation when visitors stopped for a moment on their way out, just to catch a glimpse of their image. It seemed passers by required a closer inspection of their reflection, which provided

Cedrina a chance of contact as they knelt on the soft padding to get closer to the mirror. On those occasions, Cedrina caught glimpses of human life energy and wished to prolong those short-lived encounters. How splendid it would be if even one passer-by could be open for an in-depth connection! Sighing inwardly, Cedrina was consoled with the realization that little moments of contact were, after all, better than nothing, and they certainly kept alive her hope of a human connection.

A Cold Day's
Chilly Arrival

Moving deeper into the past dream-memory on the hat rack's arrival day, Cedrina recalled daylight brighter than usual for that time of year, due of course to the glowing whiteness from the snow-filled outdoors reflecting off the mirror. She recalled missing the normal warmth from the great light, which remained hidden behind the clouds of winter and kept wakefulness somewhat shadowy, much like the lake waters during a storm. As the murky waters of the dream began to clear, a picture emerged of the Dear One stomping his feet outside the door. The thundering sound was perhaps meant as a warning before entering. It was this strange entrance, a departure from the Dear Ones' customary habit of arriving through a side door entrance that actually startled the little bench. Her dear human seemed all out of breath from carrying such a heavy load as he gingerly stomped his way into the previously quiet solitude of the alcove.

A bizarre and unusual scene ensued, with bits of snow flying over the floor and carpet along with a steady, rhythmic flow of what looked like heavy mist accompanying each breath and stomp from the Dear One. Mixed in this intriguing scene were dried leaves flying in circles around his feet that only added to the oddity of the Dear Ones' most unusual, noisy entry. At first glance, amongst the bundle of items carried, there was a long, awkward-looking stick of some kind, with strange protrusions coming out of the top. The object turned out to be a tall pole that was unceremoniously plunked in the corner of the alcove, right beside the bench. Oddly enough, this exact placing of the rack next to the little bench was accompanied by a deep sigh, followed by the most extraordinary utterance. *'There you are, together again.'* It had been spoken with firm resignation by the Dear One.

Cedrina had no recollection of connection with such a strange looking object, which emitted only icy silence, even at that time. The cool energy from the most unusual happening increased greatly to the chilly atmosphere of an already cool winter's day. It appeared that a momentous change was about to upset the perfect balance of harmony found in the confines of the little alcove's space. Secrecy now emerged as a heavy cloud engulfed the mysterious pole.

The Dear One left the room only to return with many hats in hand, and he carefully placed each one on the strange, curved branches of the mysterious pole. Its purpose was now established as that of a resting place for prized hats. This determination somewhat helped offset the first impression of being an unapproachable dark, shiny pole. A peculiar grin of satisfaction became evident as the Dear One stepped back to admire the display. A flash of something familiar surfaced for Cedrina. It had been but a momentarily glimpse of a vague awareness recollection, seemingly triggered by the grin of satisfaction radiating from her dear human. Nevertheless, the moment quickly passed, only to be replaced by her curious, deep desire to connect to this puzzling new arrival. Regrettably, that connection would not materialize, leaving Cedrina with only a hazy whisper of familiar awareness, like a distant, faint echo calling at the outer edge of memory; however, it remained blocked by a heavy mist of confusion. Perhaps one day awareness to the mystery of familiarity with the new alcove companion would come!

Moment of Reflection

The emotional ups and downs of hope<u>less</u>ness and hope<u>ful</u>ness with disappointment are a poignant reminder to the sporadic kaleidoscope of feelings we all face, with situations seemingly out of one's control.

Elation and feeling are energized with unexpected changes, yet at the same time, apprehension of an unknown future (a result of those very changes) seems a most familiar experience.

Perhaps quieting one's thoughts to one of mindfulness to the moment is a first step to pave the way for easing the tension of the unknown.

HOUSEHOLD
ENERGY SHIFT

ARRIVAL OF THE GUEST

Just like a wild summer storm from the past, a frantic liveliness replaced the previously calm and quiet of the normal household routine. Excitement charged through the home, leaving behind a new, pristine atmosphere in the household environment. This refreshing atmosphere penetrated the nooks and crannies of every room. No space was left untouched by the Dear Ones' frenzy of activity, giving the appearances of exceptional preparation and then some. Could all this be just for the arrival of the special guest? The early morning ritual of peaceful solitude in the little alcove began to take on subtle changes. It seemed this newly exhilarated household energy disrupted the usual easy flow connection between all the energy life- forms in the home.

Awareness of a diverse tone and pitch to nature sounds coming from the other side of the door did not go unnoticed. Cedrina came to realize that the Dear Ones spent a greater amount of time and energy working outside, giving the surrounding area a well-manicured appearance. All this commotion was evidence of a strong desire to have all features of their property, both inside and out, in tip-top shape. If one could believe it, even Furry Four Legs emitted a restless energy, not knowing what to do about all the fuss and bother. It seemed the tiny ball of fur also felt the effects of diminished attention from the dear humans and began spending most of the time hidden away out of sight.

Just as things started to settle, the noise level and whirl of activity was charged yet again, this time with the arrival of the special house guest from far away. Change in early morning routines was evident by the lovely aromas of meal preparation drifting throughout the house – another indication that something unusual was taking place. A steadily growing buzz of conversation with odd breakouts of laughter replaced the usual quiet hum from the rural home. It seemed that the once predictable and comforting daily routine would never again be the same. Although the Dear Ones eventually returned to a semblance of the alcove morning routine, the sporadic visits were not always together, and they did not stay as long. Cedrina noted the absence of the normal, loving energy from the Dear Ones, with the greater amounts of time spent away from their familiar surroundings.

Resignation to the transition about to take place was affirmed by passing remarks overheard from time to time between the guest and Cedrina's dear humans. While moving from one room to another, Cedrina heard words to the effect of '*huge lifestyle change*', '*must be sold with the property', 'keep or give away', and 'what will we do with this?'* It was dually noted that after each utterance, there was a long, deep sigh and quiet deliberation between the three. Uneasiness again began to take hold throughout the entire premises as it seemed the inevitable changes were taking a toll on everyone.

In spite of the adjustment difficulties, it soon became apparent that not all in the home continued to feel uneasy with the anxious energy effects in this highly charged atmosphere. One would be hard pressed not to miss a subtle difference from previous attachment and connection between Furry Four Legs and the Dear Ones. Evidently a loyalty transformation was in the works because attention had now shifted to the new arrival. The guest would often join one or both of the Dear Ones in the little alcove to discuss plans for the day's activities. This new loyalty change was becoming well established because the little fur ball now found comfort on the lap of the guest before proceeding to its normal vibrational purring.

A noteworthy alteration in daily alcove routine soon developed. The guest would enter into the space to enjoy some mid-afternoon solitude followed by Furry Four Legs, who without any hesitation became the faithful companion to the new visitor. Cedrina soon warmed to this change because the guest's presence seemed to somehow bring soothing relief to any building household agitation. The vibration from this visitor was vibrant, loving, and kind, although very much like what was emitted from the Dear Ones,

Cedrina noted an added dimension of attentiveness to the energy found in the alcove space. The possibilities for a new, meaningful connection grew stronger with each passing day. Wakefulness and dream whispers were building in intensity, seemingly derived from an unusual energy force emanating from the guest. It was this building intensity that again stimulated a passionate desire for deeper core connection within the life energy of Cedrina.

A thrilling connection and awareness response arose on a cool, damp, and drizzly spring afternoon in the little alcove. Until the guest appeared, the only sound heard after the Dear Ones left for the afternoon was the steady pitter-patter of raindrops on the outside of the front entrance window. After momentarily pausing before entering the little alcove, as if adjusting or tuning into a vibrational call of connection, the guest cautiously stepped through the doorway. She carried with her a rich blue knitted shawl along with a journal, notepad, and pen. After getting comfortable on the bench and cocooned in the shawl, the guest reached over to caress the indented marks at the base of the hat rack. It was at that exact moment of contact that the atmosphere of the room went through a subtle but noticeable change. It seemed that both the guest and Cedrina, at the very same time, sensed a loving energy deep beneath the many layers of glossy black paint. How very strange, for at that moment of awareness, just like a current of lightning, a spark of energy ran across the words carved into the backrest of the little bench.

Furry Four Legs soon arrived and curled up in its usual spot close to the guest, and immediately began a connection ritual with soft, vibrational purring. Once the purring started, the energies of the room gently entwined into a quiet stillness. Cedrina became impelled to try to connect once again with the aloof, distant hat rack. Her contact ritual began as usual, however this time Cedrina did not get very far into her appeal before a shift in response took place. Each one in the gathering became aware of a pleasant hum in the atmosphere, like a rhythmic energy pulse slowly expanding and contracting throughout the space. How very peculiar – this new energy force was in sync with the now much louder purring from Furry Four Legs. The purring became so loud and strong, in fact, that it was hard to tell if the purring was responsible for the pulsating energy, or if the energy was responsible for the rhythm of the purring. The guest, who moments before was gazing at the rack, picked up her journal and pen and began to write, all the while keeping time with the pulse of the room.

A current of the most extraordinary healing energy soon took form, laying a foundation for powerful communication never before experienced. This force created a strong connection bond between them all. Just as perplexing, in this awareness moment, the hat rack sent the much-awaited acknowledgment to Cedrina through the guest. This experience was intensified by a deeper increase of purring from Furry Four Legs, seemingly strengthening the overall connection with the unique sound and vibration emitting through its little body. Incredible compassion to and from each other was eagerly absorbed.

The only way to describe what had taken place throughout this amazing moment would be that of joyful bliss. No other words could give credence to the elation that this strange connection evoked in the little group. How fortunate that the guest was able to absorb this mystifying connection, putting it into words. From this exhilarating experience came the understanding that Cedrina's desires of expression could now come to fulfilment; the young cedar tree story would, without a doubt, be shared with any and all who would listen.

Moment of Reflection

A human desire to be heard and understood stands out as a worthy quest, providing opportunities of life fulfilment and happiness. Perhaps it is not so outlandish for other life forms to have similar dreams of expression, with the ability to connect and be part of something greater.

We have long been able to observe connection desires in our pets and livestock, and of course there are those humans that claim to actually communicate with other life energy forms on a much deeper level than normally expected.

Perhaps consideration could be made that a kinship bonding connection with other life-forms may be an integral part of the spirit of energy itself; 'like finding like' comes to mind.

DREAM MEMORIES EXPAND

A dam filled with life energy awareness had indeed burst upon Cedrina, awakening powerful dream-memories. These memories would tap into her deep energy core awareness, with new understanding aspects of growth from her past sapling and young cedar tree life learning. Clear visions of the past came flooding through as the barriers that had previously confined them to vague and fading recollections were now swept away. A memory link to cedar tree awareness of a longing to understand more about immediate surroundings was the first to surface. This deep, yearning connection was accompanied by an unquenchable curiosity while experiencing wave after wave of growing life force energy as a small red cedar tree.

Emerging awareness of a deep frustration also bubbled to the surface during the early beginnings of expansion throughout this particular dream memory. Remarkably, this visionary memory opened to an awareness of receiving soothing whispers of encouragement as a young tree, to stay strong in purpose and to be patient. Assurance was given that learning would come at the appropriate time. In the vision, Cedrina, the young sapling, was urged to trust in the soothing internal sensations that accompanied her progression of growth and expansion, moving her up and out to that of a strong, healthy young cedar. This whispered growth wisdom, passed on to the little cedar tree sprig, came from a very old, decaying tree lying on the forest floor nearby.

Cedrina, now deeply immersed in the dream-memory of early times, became aware that what was happening was not only being remembered, but was once again being experienced. Cedrina, as a bench, could once again experience the sensations of being rooted as a very young tree, desperately wanting to learn and experience what was well beyond her present boundaries of understanding. An intense curiosity and early frustration would build from what was sensed but not observed, being so tiny. She was able to comprehend a view far above and beyond the immediate surroundings, triggering more questions that stemmed from her unquenchable desire for knowledge. Her cedar tree desire for knowledge was not easily satisfied until, just as the dying tree predicted, *'Growth and expansion will bring understanding that arrives with the gift of maturity.'* The little cedar sprig would need to settle in and trust the growth process.

Cedrina, as a little cedar, also began to understand that knowledge gained from this expansion was helped along by connections to other life energies as they crossed paths. She would eventually come to realize that the more information one acquires, the more one needs to know more. An awareness of purpose slowly budded, but not fast enough to quench the deep red cedar thirst for learning. The low frequency of life energy emitting from the old, dying tree nearby was still strong enough to relay many important life messages during early growing spurts of the little cedar.

Learning took place about the life cycle connection of a cedar's increasing growth and transformation of purpose. It was a natural progression of change, even during the disintegration process that was happening with the old dying tree. This growth awareness was understood by every tree in the forest. Each tree came to the understanding that all knowledge gathered over time would in turn be passed on to satisfy the every increasing questioning that comes from younger trees during growing cycles. Awareness came to the little cedar that what was being shared during the decaying process actually starts when still upright, before a tree's mass eventually falls to the forest floor. Even after the fall, life energy continues as the once vibrant tree's decaying matter continues to offer nourishment, sanctuary, and support to all the life-forms that feed from its life energy before completing the cycle back to Mother Earth.

Each awareness lesson from the dying tree was eagerly absorbed by the inquiring energy of the little cedar. As she began listening carefully to what was being shared, her wisdom grew. With expansion and growth, the little cedar was eventually able to take in sights and sounds from other trees, including those that resided in the distance. The old, dying tree shared how life energy grew throughout a life cycle, absorbing strength and nourishment from both Mother Earth below and the great light above. Both were crucial energies that contributed to the building and expanding of wisdom taking place deep in the cedar's core and would last over vast amounts of time. There was no ending of this deep core life force coming from below and above, continuing with the ongoing seasons of growth, expansion, and energy awareness even in the times of deep winter's rest.

RED CEDAR LIFE
AWARENESS

ANCIENT CEDAR WISDOM

The little cedar received ancient knowledge of a special evergreen destiny, as a safe haven for numerous types of forest life forms. Evergreen purpose included protection from nature's seasons for those seeking shelter, easily found among thick branches during spring's awakening, summer's growth, and fall's preparation for sanctuary during the long winter. A gift of nourishment and safety were also available from a tree's outer and inner bark. Many tiny, winged, and crawling life forms could be found in the rich, nourishing outer layers of a tree. The same was true for four-legged creatures that set up home amongst its roots, which with older trees could be found both above and below the ground.

The cedar learned from the dying tree that the very energy required for growth and expansion was in turn shared outwardly within the world in which she thrived. This incredible wisdom came to be known as a collective, honoured purpose by all trees sharing life energy that would contribute to the quality of the very atmosphere, keeping all air-breathing life-forms alive.

The little cedar was just beginning to understand that a gift of sharing one's energy came in many different forms, and the knowledge being shared was only a portion of what could be learned during the ongoing seasons of life maturing that were to still come.

So much of the wisdom that came from the old tree seemed extraordinary to the little growing cedar. When the little cedar began to consider the mass of space beyond her immediate surroundings, she was filled with wonder and amazement, considering that for some energy life-forms, the tree was their entire world. Incredibly, a few tiny creatures' complete life span from energy emergence to life completion took place within the safety of the tree. To the little cedar, this purpose was considered a most glorious gift of service offered to any living thing. Once having accumulated this knowledge, viewing life as having a sacred purpose was easy. From that time on, the little cedar now knew that all life connections bring a sense of purpose that resides deep in all energy life-forms on Mother Earth.

Fascinating connection tales from an ancient dream-memory passed down from red cedar trees of long ago were also relayed to the growing cedar. She learned that ancient trees were able to keep insights and memories alive as they called out to other passing life energies, sharing stories as a means of expressing new and old acquired knowledge. In keeping with tradition, the old, dying tree shared amazing information and wisdom of how the young cedar's ancestors were able to provide service not only to the immediate surrounding life energies, but also to human life-forms many seasons in the past.

PAST PURPOSE –
SERVICE TO HUMANS

The young cedar, filled with fascinating tales of purpose, learned bit by bit from the dying tree how early humans in the surrounding area had developed tools to thin out the thick forest, and how they had made use of the giant cedars that at one time were found to be growing in abundance. The great forest trees were so thick that it seemed the great light was all but shut out by their large girth and thick branches. It was hard to comprehend how any little sapling would ever be able to absorb enough of the great light above or have room to stretch a root system to survive and grow within the density of the forest that the old tree was explaining. The little red cedar would often ponder on the information being shared, after all his energy was quickly fading, and one had to consider whether memory was also becoming distorted with the diminishing vigour that had taken place in the old one. No matter – to the young cedar, growing interest continued to increase with her ongoing maturation and growth.

The red cedar listened very carefully to these tales of old, eagerly absorbing as much as possible as the dying tree, fading faster in expression, slowly explained how these early humans did not waste any portion of the mighty cedars of the past. They used the special rot-resistant wood as a sacred gift of the red cedar. They were able to use them for floating devices to keep them safe and dry as they travelled on the lakes and rivers in the area. There was no end to the ways that the trees of old could be used, enhancing and expanding life purpose for the majestic cedars of the past. They were made into massive posts and beams for the humans' places of shelter. The sweet-smelling cedar wood was made into boxes for storage, and these humans even carved monumental poles, many of which were still standing, to declare lineage to all who came across them. These ancient humans used part of the mighty red cedar to make strange, mysterious masks to evoke energies from the spirit world. Even the inner bark of the cedar was used by weaving it into intricately patterned mats and baskets. Part of the cedar bark was made into rope and processed to make soft, warm, water-repellent clothing. Even the tree's roots were woven into watertight baskets.

These special humans held the little cedar's ancestors and their spirits' energies in very high regard, believing they held special healing and spiritual powers. They would be given names like 'long life maker', 'life giver', and 'healing woman'. *(See Footnote)*

After absorbing this ancient wisdom and brimming with wonder and newfound curiosity about this amazing connection between her ancestors and humans, the young cedar became filled with a strong desire for a similar experience. She was captivated with the shared tales of the past, and over time, the little cedar explored dream visions of ways she also could be of use to humans, similar to what the old tree had explained. This desire steadily grew as the seasons progressed, hoping and dreaming that she could go through such a transition.

Determination to experience human life energy had indeed taken deep root, and the little red cedar was sure that such an opportunity would bring a fuller understanding to a deeper meaning of connection. Could these deeply imbedded desires and dreams come true? Would she too be privileged with such an opportunity to view and connect with humans in these surroundings? It was a strange hope for the little cedar, considering it would be difficult (if not impossible) to observe a human in those early days of its young tree life. At that time, the area remained much like an untouched forest, thick and moist, covered with dense

Footnote: The ancient red cedar, Thuja plicata, specimen that survives in Catherfral Grove represents a critical species to First Nations. In her book Cedar: Tree of Life to the Northwest Coast Indians, Hilary Stewart describes how the indigenous way of life is dependent on big cedar trees.

bush and fallen, decaying trees – all sharing the space amongst the tall, stately trees that surrounded the quiet lake inlet.

Many seasons passed before the little cedar became aware of faint whispers from breezes that had travelled from afar, speaking of human habitation in the outlying areas. Most important, not long after, came news from various nearby tree whispers that human activity was heard from just across the lake. These rumours could not help but feed the little cedar's unyielding dreams of service to the unknown humans. Unfortunately, at that time she was not yet tall enough to view such activity, or sturdy enough for the larger winged creatures to perch on her outstretched branches in order to rest and share knowledge of human encounters. The little cedar became even more determined to grow tall and sturdy enough to hold the large flying creatures. What freedom they must enjoy, to soar so high above Mother Earth! What marvellous knowledge they must gather from afar! Without a doubt, she knew a day would arrive when they would find solace atop her high and mighty branches to share awareness of the expansive world they were privileged to observe and experience.

As things stood at the present, it was hard to imagine or to even suppose that a time would come for the little tree to experience human contact, let alone connection. The only life energies Cedrina presently experienced were small life-forms that made use of the nearby lake, and the smaller winged creatures that took refuge among her spindly branches from time to time. It seemed the smaller visitors stayed clear of larger creatures, knowing direct connection could possibly mean shorter life energy, so their sharing was limited. Of course, there remained connection possibilities with the elusive four-legged creatures that quickly passed, but at this particular time of the little cedar's growth and maturity, they showed little interest in sharing because they ignored all attempts of enticement by the little red cedar to drop by for a visit. The fragile cedar instinctively knew that a time would surely come when her call for attention would be answered.

Moment of Reflection

A quote easily comes to mind from the experiences expressed with understanding of purpose and desires to be of service to others. Ralph Waldo Emerson said, 'The only person you are destined to become is the person you decide to be.'

That's wise counsel when trying to find one's way in a most confusing world. Are we not all surrounded by harmony and life purpose? Is it possible to really listen with heartfelt love and appreciation for what is, and to tap into the depths of our souls, which are calling out to be heard?

> *'Your vision becomes clear when you look inside your heart. Who looks outside, dreams. Who looks inside, awakens.'* – Carl Jung

EXPANSION OF DESIRE

Cedrina, as a young maturing red cedar, learned that as time progressed, so too did her longing to connect with humans. A steady progression of growth allowing expansion, spreading outstretched branches, and collecting more and more light energy also brought awareness to other forest life-forms that would eventually view her as a strong, healthy, and mature young cedar worthy of connection. Although still hidden deep in her core, this strong human contact desire was often superseded with all the new and exciting experiences that she had derived from increasing opportunities with new forest life energy sharing connections.

The growth of experiences during the time of expansion brought interest, pleasure, and purpose to daily life as a special evergreen cedar. Gathering knowledge from the surrounding life energies took a great deal of focus, temporarily taking precedence over the unproductive dreams of what could be. There was much to learn from the nature world of the forest and lake area. During this time of growth, the red cedar learned how growth and location had an effect on life energy experiences that highly influenced other life-forms' connection possibilities in the immediate surroundings. The little cedar came to realize that not all cedars have the same growth potential.

Cedrina found growing up close enough to the shoreline offered but a glimpse of the lake that would improve with her growth potential. The little tree's unique growing position offered a great vantage point to observe all types of life forms that lived in and close by the water. This was a great advantage point for the magnificent flying creatures, called the great ones that made use of the lake as a play and hunting area, especially in the warmer, wakeful growing seasons. Many amusing and captivating interactions between all the land and water creatures that made use of the lake created a peaceful location for the little cedar.

Interesting news could be gleaned from the odd piece of driftwood that would wash up on shore as a gift from the lake. During occurrences of driftwood connection, the little cedar was provided delightful information while absorbing uniquely shared life cycle stories. She could also look forward to driftwood tales collected from the four-legged land creatures, as well as small, winged creatures exploring the shoreline. Many of the creatures would stop for a moment on their way back to resting areas, but before leaving they'd pass on what was learned from their foraging adventures.

There were special moments of high tide stories gleaned from a most exciting early spring greeting. Spring was a time when the water level rose due to the melting snow from the surrounding mountains. Periods with fast-flowing currents that entered the little lake frequently brought new and exciting biological diversity. Especially interesting were the tales shared by the large, old logs from farther afield, once they washed up close enough for firsthand connection. It was a time of abundant awareness opportunities from what could be learned throughout any log's tree life cycle, including interesting water adventures that they were more than willing to share. Yes, early spring certainly was established as the perfect awakening time in order to grow in height, breadth, and unique opportunity time to store new learning.

In those early times of maturing, there were no signs of 'two legs', a name that many forest creatures liked calling humans when sharing life awareness stories. To the majority of smaller creatures, humans were found to be extremely peculiar and very unpredictable beings. It simply did not matter to the red cedar that many of the stories shared contained unsettling, murky awareness of humans. Cedrina, even in tree-form viewed this murkiness as fear stories, and frankly, fear was something that the little cedar had long ago overcome. No matter the implication of darkness to any interactive story, visions of a time of wonderful human connection remained strong and sound. Thanks to the dying tree and ancestral wisdom stories shared, the young tree was left with unmistakable knowledge to the existence of loving, caring humans.

In spite of tales of encounters with humans from the surrounding area being few and far between, it did nothing to deter the little cedar from belief that they would one day come. Her certainty of the eventuality of human arrival was reinforced by whispers from distant trees relaying news of what was taking place, with the forest area thinning happening not too far away. The thinning process taking place was explicitly for camping sites used by the humans. Oddly enough, whispers from some areas stopped altogether, only to be taken up by eerie or ghostly information from howling winds that had passed through. The little red cedar found the hollowness from the winds passing through some surrounding forest areas and arriving with almost complete silence of forest life energy was indeed hard to comprehend.

Cedrina found it difficult to fathom that so many life-forms and foliage simply disappeared, leaving only short stubs where once magnificent trees stood. Admittedly, there was some disquieting energy that would accompany those particular reports that would —only momentarily mind you - create concern to the little cedar. Determined to remain forever optimistic, Cedrina would turn the story to a positive spin and associate the disappearance with some type of glorious service such as her great red cedar ancestors had experienced. After all, what better fate could there be than fulfilling a desire for human energy connection? The little cedar remained adamant that this type of service ending would be like a dream come true, and she was certain this desire was connected to cedar tree destiny. But for now, the little tree would need to remain content with bits and fragments of news about humans from the winds and the rumours from flying creatures that stopped at the water's edge. At least at this particular dream-memory time, what future path that magical journey of connection took would have to remain a mystery, at least for the present.

Moment of Reflection

If it were not for deep desires filled with curiosity for the unknown, then perhaps expansion of growth and the accumulation of knowledge would be hampered.

Maturity provides more opportunities to grow in knowledge, arriving from inside and outside of one's immediate environment. After all, insight is acquired with connections made while exploring the environment and sharing life experiences with others.

One could conclude, therefore, that in spite of what is learned and accepted as truth and wisdom from others, there remains a longing to know more, especially when living in a world of mystery, change, and challenge that calls out to be explored and appreciated.

A UNIQUE ALCOVE ADDITION

DELIGHTFUL NEW ENCHANTMENT

It was such a splendid and delightful moment shared by the energy connection of the little foursome, made up of the guest, Furry Four Legs, hat rack, and Cedrina. In fact, it was so intense that time had slipped by with no indication of even passing. The guest, now having stiffened fingers from writing, left the alcove waving and shaking out hand and finger cramps, followed closely behind by Furry Four Legs in the hopes of receiving some much-needed nourishment. The little bench was left wondering whether the magical moment that had taken place would be repeated. How amazing to have all those dream memories become so vivid and alive, so clear and strong, leaving no doubt to past life energy as a growing red cedar. The experience had provided so much reassurance that life was good, and there was no room left for the slowly fading hazy memories of the past. No matter what came next, the experience shared during that special moment in time would remain forever magical. Cedrina was caught up in the euphoric experience with the hat rack, and she wondered if the awareness blocking that previously surrounded the rack too had ended, making a way for easy connection.

It was much later in the day that the rain stopped and the alcove returned to its normal, tranquil state. Awareness of a chill in the air became evident, not only due to the coolness of the oncoming evening, but also from Cedrina's disenchantment with the return of icy cool silence emanating from the hat rack. This now unexpected silence was contributed greatly to a chill right to the core, chasing away any residue of previous connection euphoria. Hopelessness was quickly gaining control, overriding the briefest of moments where the little bench had rejoiced in the belief that the muted silence of the hat rack would be forever gone. How disappointing to have experienced a strong attachment in the magic of such an enchanting moment.

It was unfathomable at this time that such a sensation of oneness could so quickly disappear, however Cedrina considered the occurrence as a most important sharing experience, in spite of the realization that it would likely be relegated to that of a magical dream. How strange it was that the hat rack could evoke such strong reactions from the little bench in the first place. Perhaps one day Cedrina would become content and at peace with the inner conflict that took place from this dreary and mysterious hat rack. Could it be possible that little cedar bench was actually feeling miffed?

Adding disappointment to the present gloomy atmosphere, there seemed to be no sign of the Dear Ones returning, leaving the bench wondering whether they would come back at all. Missing a loving presence was short-lived, however, because later in the evening, the guest returned, seemingly on a mission. Unsure of the purpose, Cedrina became curious as the guest twisted a small hook into the wood frame of the window. A most peculiar object now dangled in front of the window pane, slowly swaying on the hook. Cedrina was intrigued by the object's appearance, which had a diamond shape and unique sparkle; it turned out to be a small glass container filled with water. A new mystery was indeed unfolding! How strange to hang such an endearing object that could possibly impede the full impact of the great light's early morning rays.

After what had happened earlier this day with the vivid connection experience, the object was perhaps a mysterious gesture of appreciation in the form of a sparkling new addition to the alcove. It certainly added to the oddity of what had taken place earlier. To Cedrina, one of the many charms regarding humans was not really being able to predict what they were going to do next. In the days of tree life during moments of human energy contact, a huge portion of insight to human purpose and demeanour would forever remain a mystery to Cedrina. After observing numerous humans over her life span, at least thus far, the little bench was beginning to find understanding why the four-legged creatures from the forest were so jittery.

Cedrina did not have any past dream-memory whispers that would have prepared her for the vibrant energy she experienced through the guest each day. It seemed that ever since the guest had arrived, the household atmosphere was transformed and would remain in a constant flow of change, which was turning out to be quite the enthralling experience. There was something magical and mystifying about it all, leaving one to ponder with eager anticipation what on earth would the next moment bring? In spite of the coolness of the evening, the little bench was sure that for the next while, a very adventurous journey was to be had – at least, as long as the guest remained a part of the household energy.

Fascination soon kicked in with a slight flash of reflection coming from the new water-filled container, which it seemed easily captured a glimmer from the moonlit night sky. Cedrina was quite familiar with water energy, and the bench felt somehow comforted by the gentle stimulation of dream-memories that began bubbling to the surface with each moonlit flicker reflecting through the water glass. Strange, indeed, thought Cedrina, because previously her dream-memories were only awakened by the early morning light streaming through the windows. It seemed now that the lesser light also had awakening power. Water energy recollections of learning during cedar life energy growth by the lake now seemed ripe and ready to burst to the surface. The little bench instinctively knew that in the days to come, life would be even more thrilling and filled with new insights emerging from dream-memory whispers, no matter the placement of the great light. The heavy silence of night soon engulfed the household as a new depth of dream state for Cedrina soon took hold.

WATER ENERGY AWARENESS

Cedrina again became enmeshed in a dream recollection as a little cedar tree nestled in the outer edge of the forest. Sure enough, she revisited sights and sounds of water creatures. These memories were filled with delightful energy actions taking place during the precious time by the lake. Some of the most enjoyable memories stemmed from observing the interaction and connection with underwater creatures and the mighty flying creatures, which for some reason were not able to mix all that well. She watched as great battles for supremacy would take place between the two; neither could cope for very long in each other's worlds. Amusing memories surfaced with scenes of the underwater life-forms being swooped up by the large flying creatures circling just above the surface of the little lake.

During a most amusing lake observation, an unusual sight with a battle of wills took place, while the little red cedar was enjoying the versatility and strength of a large flying creature on the hunt for food. It seems the mighty one had captured a very large water creature and was having difficulties getting it up and away.

A battle of strength resumed as this winged one was determined to hang on to such a large catch. The next best plan of action, if one could believe, was to swim to shore with its prize tightly grasped in its talons. It did seem touch-and-go for a bit, with two mighty energies in their battle for supremacy of strength and endurance. There were moments when it seemed the water creature might actually win its struggle for freedom, as the winged creature slowly sank into the water. However, the water creature was unable to hold its strength long enough against the determination of the great one's ability to keep a tight grip. The young cedar watched in amazement as powerful wings began brushing the water like paddles, slowly inching them closer to the water's edge. It soon became apparent who lost; after a long and strenuous battle, the water creature finally gave in to its fate. The antics of this survival drama brought a great deal of attention from other forest creatures. Many awareness stories would soon be shared of the unfathomable prowess of this great flying creature.

Another joy-filled memory emerged, involving a large, mature underwater creature being unceremoniously dropped from the sky. The young cedar was elated with the opportunity of such a close water creature encounter. It was so close, in fact, that it created a soft, swaying movement in one of Cedrina's branches as it passed by, on its way to become earthbound and landing with a great thud at the base of little tree. It seemed that the talons of this particular great winged creature had lost the tight grip on its prize. A strange sight indeed, observing the frantic movements of the water creature flopping around on the forest floor, picking up unfamiliar dirt and dried leaves. In spite of such dire circumstances, a very intense moment of connection took place before the life energy of the water creature expired. Not to be deterred by circumstances, it seemed the noble creature wanted to make sure that its own accumulated knowledge was shared.

Amazing awareness of underwater scenes from the nearby lake quickly became apparent to the young cedar. Surprisingly, during only a moment of the brief connection, a great deal of information was quickly absorbed from this single energy life-form, filling the little cedar with tremendous energy awareness. The dying creature overflowed with knowledge from various underwater species passing through its territory, and before being swooped up again by the large winged creature, this awareness of large oceans and vast seas was passed on to the cedar tree. Visions of underwater hills and valleys teeming with untold varieties of water creatures gracefully moving in the depths was only part of what was shared in that magical moment of time.

Many of these old underwater creatures living in the larger oceans held much wisdom, just like the ancestors of the young red cedar. This energy connection sharing was filled with amazing water life forms in all shape and sizes. The cedar marvelled at the lack of restrictions in movement during the creature's life span. What a glorious feeling it must have been for this aquatic life form to have lived with such freedom! Amazingly, it was able to glide to and fro towards new adventures, gathering information moment by moment. There were many wonders to behold in a world that was invisible to all but those who lived in its depths. A truly mystical moment of connection, experienced by the little tree of the past, was again taking place within the core of Cedrina the cedar bench.

This magical, moonlit night brought to life numerous fading memories from her past with varying types of life forms enjoying a bounty of both nourishment and pleasure, provided as gifts from the lake. Amongst this diverse water energy was a recollection of a family of very playful otters frolicking about in the water. At times they would be leisurely floating on top of the water without a care, and in a flash of a moment, they'd begin chasing each other above and below the lake surface. The little cedar was enchanted with the scene, and she watched in amazement at the small aquatic creatures that were so at home both above and below the lake surface, and how they held on to each other to keep from drifting away as they floated on a tranquil blanket of water. What was most amusing to the little tree about this family of otters was observing them snacking while floating on their backs: they opened crustaceans that had been retrieved from the lake's bottom. The noise they made during this most amusing habit would echo across the water as they used small rocks to crack open the outer shells in order to feast on the tender morsels found inside.

Soon to follow the enchanting otter scene was a lively and picturesque scene of a pair of cranes staying close to the reeds at the water's edge. This unique recollection came swooping in amongst the water dream–memories that were taking place, and surreal flashes of the past bubbled to the surface. This memory was bringing pure delight as Cedrina revisited the captivating moment: the pair flew over the water and made their strange sounds before landing near their precious nesting site. The little cedar wondered whether the pair being viewed in this revealing memory was about the same pair that would return each spring season, settling themselves amongst the tall marsh reeds at the end of the little lake.

Another water memory that quickly surfaced was amongst the recollections of the pleasant practices of ducks. She found great pleasure watching them dive in search for food, sometimes disappearing completely in the water's depth. Other times, in the shallower areas of the lake, they would dive for food with tails bobbing on the surface before quickly popping up after achieving the goal of finding nourishment from the lake bottom. These particular energy creatures would most often be found in groups, keeping a watchful eye on the little ones eagerly following and mimicking their actions. Once the young ones were ready, many practice runs of flying over the lake surface together would take place. It seemed they preferred to eat, play, and sleep in groups, just like the geese, or what the cedar like to call them, honking long necks, that dropped by for a visit to the little lake from time to time.

Not to be forgotten in among the moonlit recollections, were the underwater creatures themselves, flipping up into the air in order to catch the tiny flying creatures swarming just above. It seemed as if the tiny insects were taunting the underwater creatures. This leaping action would end with a soft plopping sound as the creatures dropped back into the depths. The larger ones, however, managed quite a splash before returning to the mysterious underwater world. These water energy actions would often take place at dusk, in the magical moments when the great light slowly slipped behind the surrounding mountains, making way for the lesser light to weave its tranquil spell of peace for all forest life energies around the lake area. It would soon be time for the night foragers to make their presence known.

Astonishing water memories splashed about in the dreams of Cedrina that magical moonlit night, and they slowly come to an end with a quiet reflection scene of a large, full moon high above, sending it small but bright light to glisten over the waters of the serene mountain lake. Cedrina slipped into a deep and peaceful sleep, which was understandable with so many dream-memories overflowing with pleasure and filling her with forgotten awareness experiences found amongst the natural surroundings and past moments of contentment.

Moment of Reflection

Memories, like energy whispers, delve deep into consciousness to bring up life experiences, thoughts, or ideas to the forefront.

How amazing it is that stimulation from the simplest or even slightest of our senses – like, taste, smell, or a mere flicker of light – may trigger a most pleasant memory of the past to explore and enjoy it yet again.

Of course, there are those not-so-pleasant challenging memories that are triggered and that may or may not be welcomed.

'Deep at the center of my being is an Infinite Well of Love.' – Louise L. Hay

EXPLORING LIGHT ENERGY

ENERGY GIFT OF
PASSION – TO BE

The mystical night filled with delightful water dreams came to an abrupt end with a flash of intense energy bursting into the little alcove. A distinct change of energy awakened Cedrina to awe-inspiring early morning light, filling her to the brim with astonishing energy. The delightful rays grew in intensity as they expanded into passionate, deep, and vibrant shades of red. Weaving a magical spell, the great light beamed through the window with light rays filtering through the little glass container. As a gift, the water prism reflected a magnificent red glow that slowly filled the alcove space. Cedrina had awakened to a magical dance of crimson light.

The enchantment of the red glow intensified as it bounced around the room between the glass container and mirror. The dance, like a vibrant light energy show, sent a mystifying, passion-filled energy deep within the core of the little bench. Along with this most unusual display, early life beginnings came flooding back, taking Cedrina on an embryonic memory in a new birth journey. Through this birth dream memory, she was able to once again experience awareness of thrusting and bursting from a once calm reassurance of quiet entombment, enclosed in a tiny cedar seed shell. This new birth could be likened to a beam of energy that moved her violently from a surreal reverie found in a warm, damp, and silent tomb, only to be replaced by a tremendous vibrational surge that caused the tiny shell to burst open, exposing the delicate seed within.

A sense of urgency immediately took hold of the seedling, urging life energy to quickly reach deeper for much-needed nourishment as she softly landed on the forest floor. It seemed but a flash of a moment where tiny root tentacles began a quest for attachment to something soft and moist making the urgent connection that could only be found deep within Mother Earth. One could wonder how this dancing spark of vibrant red light is able to bring energy awareness to Cedrina's deep core cedar past of a slowly budding life and the deep, embedded memory of seed time. Some things remain a mystery, especially life as a tiny seed cradled in moist, decaying matter coming forth and filled with an important urge of survival and safety. For the first time, Cedrina became aware of the growing flow of energy that brought her into a world filled with wonder, which it seemed was also tied to her constantly growing life awareness.

'For a seed to achieve its greatest expression, it must come completely undone. The shell cracks, its insides come out and everything changes. To someone who doesn't understand growth, it would look like complete destruction.'

— *Cynthia Occe*

It was amazing that this early awareness was actually awakened by the intriguing energy from the water prism that had been hung in the window by the guest. It seemed that the most magnificent presence of the prism would now enable the great light to display hidden rays of colour – the catalyst for an abundance of pleasure yet to come. After experiencing the amazing red energy gift, Cedrina also became more fully aware of the importance of the red stain ingrained deep into her core consciousness, providing specific purpose to the tiny tree's very existence.

Cedrina again experienced the new ebb and flow to early energy dreams of her tree life – slowly expanding and struggling to establish a strong, purposeful existence in a sea of thick green foliage covering the forest floor. Memories surfaced of an increasing root system reaching deep into the earth in search of a continuous flow of life energy and drawing it up into a divine conscious core. As a cedar tree, awareness of life with seedling energy expansion was the actual foundation of her life energy, allowing steady growth in order to experience other forest life energies in her immediate surroundings.

For Cedrina, in this magical here and now moment with vibrant, passionate red colour dancing around the little alcove, she as a bench could again sense part of herself sinking deep into the earth below, stimulating a memory awareness of being rooted and taking hold. This understanding of life energy beginnings, previously long forgotten and hidden deep in her cedar core, was received in appreciation and humbly accepted as a gift from the newest addition to the little alcove. During this passion-filled moment of attentiveness, Cedrina marvelled at the wonder of it all, finally understanding that dreams of the past were more than wistful dreams of imagination; they were real memories all, part of the unique turn of events to the life span of a single red cedar tree.

The red cedar bench pondered on the miraculous energy from the effect of this glass container, and declared Prism Presence to be its calling. Anticipating the future colour energy experiences to come, Cedrina was certain that an abundance of joy would be shared amongst this unique group of companions gathering to experience the prism's glowing effects within the quiet solitude of this space. Brimming with passion and awareness, she was now able to have new and intuitive appreciation for all that had taken place from her past life beginnings leading up to the precious connection experiences with the Dear Ones, and on to the magic and wonder of the present moment. This knowledge alone would chase away all nagging doubts for the future. Cedrina was convinced that there was much more to come, and that a strong connection to share the past and present was so close at hand. The future was filled with incredible possibilities!

Right on cue, the guest returned, notebook and pen in hand; Furry Four Legs was close at her heels. The guest stopped for a moment at the doorway to enjoy the special effects of the prism and absorb the warm red glow before settling in the usual comfy spot on the bench. A feeling of light, joyful energy was evident by the pleasurable smile that slowly turned into a broad grin of deep satisfaction for the guest while she gazed at the glass prism. Even the leap onto the bench by Furry Four Legs seemed lighter than usual. Not surprisingly, after settling into the delightful energy awareness, all four of the companions were joyfully absorbed with a strong urge to be rooted.

This moment was also a means for the hat rack to make a connection with the bench, and intertwining with the dream-memory of reaching deep into Mother Earth was a shared experience. Rising from its usual spot while nestled close to the guest, Furry Four Legs made a soaring leap, landing softly to the floor on all fours while gazing at the little glass water prism. The guest slowly uncurled herself from a cosy position, planting both feet firmly on the floor as if to become rooted. With tear-filled eyes and hands clasped together over her heart, her mind opened to a surge of energy that only Mother Earth could provide during this inspiring moment. She instinctively knew that the depth of what was taking place was due to the combined energies in the alcove space creating an undeniable awareness to a most precious moment of oneness.

A strong, chainlike response to the most unusual connection began with the transfer of early life dream-memories from Cedrina directly to the guest, who was now vigorously writing, eager to make the most of the moment not knowing how long it would last. A smooth flow of writing continued for a spell even after the vibrancy of colour began to fade. Intrinsic awareness immediately developed between members of the little group as each adjusted to what was happening, fully understanding that the experience was indeed the result of a unique combination of life energies in response to the precious reflection of colour as a gift of prism presence.

Of course, this moment could not take place without the essential contribution of the great light's energy rays arriving at a most specific seasonal moment in time. A strong sense of pure harmony stayed with the little bench for quite some time. Earlier, Cedrina had been totally absorbed with the possibilities of an increasing energy connection with the hat rack while basking in the vibrant glow of colour, even before the other two companions had arrived. As difficult to comprehend as it was, the energy gift of red left little doubt for her that the familiarity experienced between the two alcove companions would be ongoing and intuitively; without any doubt, she knew a breakthrough was about to take place.

Nature Energy
Uncovered

Once the red light energy settled and the dream-memories were written, the guest went over to the window and reached up to the little prism to give it a twist. Happy to oblige, the prism joyfully provided a delightful exhibit of rainbow lights flashing around the room. The reflection effects were indeed a splendid example of an unexpected colour display from the great light's change in position as it rose higher in the sky. The movement of the lights flashing around the room fascinated Furry Four Legs, and with gleeful attention, it began chasing and leaping in the hopes of capturing one of the evasive lights.

It was at the precise moment, during a race and flying leap to catch one of the magical little lights, the tiny furry mass had managed to create a great collision. The hat rack toppled and landed with a thud. A most amazing occurrence took place as the guest hurriedly set the rack back up to its usual position. Startled by the resulting commotion and wasting no time, Furry

Four Legs quickly scampered out of the room while the guest proceeded to check for any damage. Upon close inspection, it seemed a piece of the outer layer of paint had become loose, leaving a large crack running down the long pole. Running a hand down the damage brought about a momentarily sense of dread as a large paint chip broke away and unceremoniously fell to the floor. There was now a gaping scar on the polished surface, exposing a portion of the pole's wood grain. Total astonishment replaced any feeling of dread as the newly exposed wood grain amazingly turned out to be identical to the beautiful graining found on the red cedar bench!

What happened next was just as exhilarating. Warm energy, coming in slow, spiralling waves, was detected flowing outward from the exposed portion of the pole to the little bench. These waves, immediately detected by Cedrina, were extraordinarily familiar. How peculiar – it seemed that the damage from the fall had miraculously enabled a sought-after connection by releasing a portion of the life energy trapped behind layers of glossy paint. Awareness blossomed between the two life energies, with the realization that the feeling of familiarity was indeed partly due to the same type of wood grain, from the same era of time, and even perhaps from the very same lakefront area. And yet there still remained a clouded mystery of origins, leaving little doubt that there was still more to uncover.

Questions soon formed much quicker than any satisfactory answer could arrive. How could this be possible? How did this deduction so easily slip by the little bench for so long? Would this life energy mystery of the two companions and the strong connection ever be solved? The little bench wistfully wondered whether future dream-memories, whispered in the early dawn, would bring about the answers to this mysterious turn of events.

Dream Door Awakening

Reflecting on all that had taken place since arriving; the guest was now able to surmise a magical quality to recent happenings. What was now being experienced felt very much like stepping through a threshold where one's eyes opened to a magical place filled with new and exciting, albeit mysterious, energy connection possibilities. This was a truly astonishing turn of events, considering that this type of occurrence had never before been experienced by her. It was while pondering this unusual experience that a literal dream-memory from the past came flooding back to the guest.

A recollection surfaced regarding a reoccurring dream – or perhaps it was more of a vision – which had started in the early days of adulthood. This ongoing dream would reappear throughout her life at the most unexpected times. The dream was made up of a most unusual house surrounded in a heavy mist that kept the house almost hidden and difficult to describe in any detail except the front door. The front door was old with aged wood that shone through the mist, giving one a deep sense of agelessness as a beckoning entrance. It was while peering through the mist to get a better view that she suddenly found herself stepping through the slowly opening front door only to find she was standing in a hall entrance. This entrance led to a room containing an unfathomable number of closed and opened doors. Finding oneself in such an observing position in the dream was a bit unnerving; creating confusion after having stepped into what seemed an empty room. Curiously, proceeding to walk towards a few of the opened doors merely led to new and unexplored empty rooms.

As the dream continued over the years, the guest, in the dream, would always find herself standing in the middle of an unexplored room surrounded with many more intriguing doors along the walls. Each door was completely different in appearance and called out for attention. If she approached any one of the doors in order to explore, some were found wide open, beckoning easy entrance, but she found others were halfway open, showing little resistance to opening further. A few of the doors were only slightly ajar, requiring effort to open enough to squeeze through. Still others were tightly closed, requiring a great deal of energy and strength to gain entrance. Many of the dream doors were firmly shut, and although they seemingly were not locked, it required far too much energy to gain entrance.

What was most amazing about this house of doors was the realization that many doors were actually locked with no means of opening without a key. Of course the guest did not know where the key was hiding, which left her to question why they were in the dream in the first place. Whenever this dream surfaced, there was a most persuasive urge to try all the doors in sight; however frustration would quickly arise because the most compelling ones would not budge. While fully in this dream state, there was an indication of stepping over the threshold of a door, and at other times finding herself already in a room with no recollection of entering. Each time she revisited the dream, there followed a sense of being in a completely different room from the last, never returning to the previous one.

Through the years, she revisited this dream with a great deal of reflection that led to an understanding that although each of the accessible rooms was found to be empty, each space had much to reflect upon. If dreams are truly an extension of one's own self, then stepping through an opened door into a new, unexplored room always seemed to coincide with a new phase of personal awareness taking place during specific life transitions, and they were closely tied to personal questioning about what was transpiring. Once a new life awareness or connection was made to a specific door in the dream, a spiritual expansion and feeling of fulfilment in heart and mind soon followed.

What was so amazing about this personal dream-memory was the realization that as time passed, tightly closed or locked doors changed. It seemed the change took place either slowly over time or suddenly in a particular moment, becoming much easier to access.

There was always a sense of a forward motion with each visit to the dream. The dream never faded in intensity or in memory in spite of the passing of time, even in the later stages of her life.

How delightful to find that what was taking place in the little alcove was like stepping through one of her dream doors. It seemed at this moment in time that the dream door led into a room filled with magical energy. With each connection experience taking place, a new cherished memory was made, filling the connecting room in the dream to be explored at a later date. Today's gift was most assuredly based on a sense of solid grounding and being able to once again visit the unusual dream with feet firmly planted on the dream room floor.

The gift of energy light and colour experienced this early morning was for the guest, tied to an understanding of the chakra energy system. Most assuredly, a balancing with the first root chakra had indeed taken place for each of the companions with this experience, leaving each eagerly anticipating and wondering what was to follow.

Moment of Reflection

*Red: 'The Base (root) Chakra Survival/Grounding/
Stability gravitation drawing into a point of trust
and self preservation, root support, desire to be in the
physical world' (www.expressionofspirit.com).*

To Be

*This root energy experience leaves one to ponder on possibilities
that a common, universal energy flow moving through a life
and down into Mother Earth, then back again, may indeed be
happening through all life-forms.*

*The unique, repetitive dream experience with the house of
doors is a reminder of human curiosity and the express need
for the awareness of moving forward.*

*The following words of affirmation come to mind with the
chakra experience and the dream.*

*'Divine right action is always taking place in my life. Only
good comes from each experience. I move forward in life with
joy and with ease.' – Louise L. Hay, You Can Heal Your Life*

ENERGY GIFT OF
PLEASURE – TO FEEL

A new day arrived, with early morning rays finding the familiar pathway through the windows of the little alcove space. As usual, the room was filled with a light energy of comfort, and just as the previous day, another amazing gift of colour appeared from the little prism. In this light energy moment, the space took on a pleasing atmosphere from the reflected light with a sensual deep orange hue. This superb rich colour reached into all corners of the little room as a warm, soothing glow. The warmth of energy from this gift of colour triggered a moment of great pleasure as Cedrina slipped yet again into dream-memory of tree life as a young cedar sapling.

This dream whisper of energy growth found Cedrina in sapling time and in the midst of becoming aware, for the first time, of very small, fast-moving, four-legged creatures entering her immediate surroundings. These little creatures moved with tails standing upright as if reaching towards the light above. They were busy exploring the surrounding brush and foliage in search of food, moving steadily in short spurts towards the delicate sapling. After each little running spurt, they would pause and take a few quick sniffs before coming to a full stop (as if frozen to the spot and waiting for the all-clear signal from the leader) and then proceeding with another little running spurt. The movement became much like a ritualistic routine made up of a running spurt, pause and sniff, freeze, and move again, all the while inching closer to the tiny cedar. The tiny sapling found a heightened curiosity while regarding such unusual movements and at the same time sense of satisfaction with being noticed. However, this satisfaction quickly turned to moments of anxiety and fear for the tiny sapling as it was the beginning of becoming aware of danger in her immediate surroundings.

The young sapling learned quickly that the quiet bubble of early growth and the sense of solitude were soon to be shared with a variety of life energies. Her immediate surroundings were turning out to be a place of shelter for small life-forms in search of safety, comfort, and nourishment that could only be found amongst abundant plant stems from the forest floor foliage. The fragile sapling felt an immediate rush of panic with the first sharp pokes to its delicate life form. This new type of awareness stemmed from one of the creatures testing the sapling as a source of nourishment with a few sniffs and a nip or two, leaving the tiny cedar with some anxious survival moments.

It was in this panic-riddled state that the little sapling also became aware of a young birch tree nearby. While desperately searching for reassurance that what was happening would not lead to her demise, the tiny sapling turned her awareness to the young birch as a possible means of comfort. It seemed odd that she had not noticed the birch earlier, especially as it stood fairly close and was taller within the surrounding shrubbery. It actually provided the sapling with a great deal of protection from the harsher elements of early spring during this season of growth. The young birch was much smaller in comparison to the older trees that encircled them both. The surroundings most assuredly would have eventually been noticed during those early days of budding awareness, however at this particular time, the frightened sapling was grateful for a chance to connect to a nearby, reassuring presence.

The young birch quickly sensed the urgent call stimulating the beginnings of the important connection. Just as the little cedar sapling franticly tuned in to the young birch tree energy, the young birch began to absorb much of the anxious energy emanating from the sapling's fragile core. This anxiety-riddled energy reminded the young birch of its own beginnings not so very long ago, and it fully understood the importance of providing relief to the tiny cedar's mushrooming awareness of fear. Once the connection was complete, the little sapling immediately felt a strong, calming energy as crucial information was transferred. The sapling quickly learned how best to deal with the intensity and discomfort being experienced.

The knowledge gathered from this soothing energy connection became the catalyst used to encourage strength and growth from that time forward. The sapling was instructed to focus on a strong, natural urge to stretch towards the great light above. Although slow at first, the realization came that in the very act of stretching towards the light, comfort would soon return. Within this comfort was a delightful awareness that the warmth emanating from the great light also provided life force energy to promote significant expansion during the warm growing season cycles. The young sapling was encouraged to trust in this growth energy, which would provide strength and life maturity as it did for all trees. For the first time, the cedar sapling experienced great pleasure within the boundaries of this exchange, and her anxious energy was all but removed and replaced with a fresh awareness of available strength hidden within her strong urge to stretch and grow. What was learned was soon considered by the sapling as a gift of wisdom ensuring pleasant survival in those early stages of growth.

This type of natural progression and reaching out for awareness connection soon became a part of the growth cycles throughout the little cedar's natural life span. Over the years, the birch often had to pacify a fast-growing curiosity that seemed to accompany the rapid growth of this cedar sapling. Many times there would be a need for reminders that the majority of early adventures and learning would come from the awe and wonder to be found in the natural surroundings. The little sapling would merely need to remain open and receptive to what came and be willing to freely explore what each connection moment brought forth.

And so it seemed that the energy memory from this gift of the orange light seeping into the core of Cedrina stimulated yet again great pleasure from expansion and new understanding during the growing seasons. New whispered memories of her budding branches surfaced. As they were newly formed, the branches would immediately reach out to catch more of the light rays, absorbing all the spectrum of energy and colour that came from the great light. They were found to grow in spurts, similar to the movement of the funny little creatures with the high-flying tails. She later learned that these quirky little creatures were named chipmunks by the humans.

Cedrina was sure that this mysterious, unknown orange spectrum from the light energy entering her core was responsible for the softening of the deep red streaks developing within her. She found that during her growth, absorbing these rays as a gift from the great light developed in the form of a special resistance. Soon the little tree would give off a particular aroma as a repellent, keeping many creatures from feasting on the life force within her core. This red cedar resistance would be recognized by most energy life-forms that came under its bough, and by those that partook of nourishment on the outer layer of her protective bark covering.

Returning now to the present moment of the alcove, Cedrina felt a familiar influence from this pleasurable gift of orange energy, opening a deeper understanding to the early growth and maturing years of the past. There was a strong recollection to the sensation of frustration that would resurface from time to time in those growing seasons. It was becoming evident that frustration was most assuredly due to many of the unknowns in her life and a lack of understanding of what was sensed but not observed, such as life energy beyond her immediate surroundings or connection influence. In tree form, this frustration, at least in part, did not have the same opportunities as the older and much taller trees. It was all too apparent to the curious cedar that others were privileged and able to store greater knowledge of the world that surrounded them. This fact alone created much of her frustration, and she wanted to know more than what was possible at each stage of growth.

Cedrina also recalled that in spite of being unsure of the unknown, there were moments of pure pleasure in these early growth stages. She had great anticipation of reaching the mighty heights of her ancestors, along with untold enjoyment that was sure to be had from future energy connections that would inevitably take place. As expected with growth the ability to absorb information during the fleeting moments of interesting life-forms passing brought her much satisfaction. By following the advice and understanding from the young birch tree, the little sapling became well rooted in understanding and acceptance that each new life experience equalled new appreciation and pleasure from all that would eventually cross her path.

Rainbow Arcs

Upon arrival at the little alcove, the guest emitted a long, deep sigh of appreciation while basking in the lovely orange glow in the short time before it started to dissipate. With a hand over her heart and with her eyes closed, she enjoyed a moment of exquisite pleasure that radiated from deep within her soul. Adding a steady and strong vibration to this pleasurable scene was Furry Four Legs, rubbing up against her legs as a welcoming jester, all the while purring loudly and drawing the others deeper into the euphoric energy that intertwined them all. The rays of the great light began to change position, causing a variance in the prism's presentation of reflection. The previous orange glow was now replaced by miniature rainbows moving slowly throughout the room. A most delightful atmosphere emerged with a charming display of light rays as reminders of the pleasing moments in the past observing rainbows.

For Cedrina, this multicolour light display brought about joyful memories of similar colourful rainbows arcing high in the sky over the lake where she once resided. A recollection soon surfaced from the teachings of the old, dying tree about an ancient awareness of the colourful arc of light, accepted in the forest as a gift from what is known as a creative life force. This colourful gift was often observed following a tremendous storm passing through the area, much like a calling card reminder as it signalled time to ponder again on the ancient awareness tale passed down from generation to generation. The tale was about high waters that covered much, if not all, of the land in the distant past. It was understood that these waters even rose to the tops of the surrounding mountains, destroying all tree life energy in its depth. It had long been accepted that the first time the arch of colours appeared was just after the great flood. From that time forward, the arc high above was viewed as a significant sign that such a flood would never again take place. It mattered not if this tale was true, because each and every time the rainbow appeared; pleasure from the view alone was always considered a gift of great promise and beauty.

Breaking the joy-filled silence, these words tumbled from the lips of the guest. *'I am so glad I followed my intuition to come for this visit, which has opened a new door of insight to energy connection.'* She then quickly settled into her usual cosy position, curled up on the bench and writing commenced. Only the steady, soft, rhythmic sound of constant writing was heard from that moment on, with the exception of the odd pause of quiet contemplation taking place while absorbing all the new energy connection information being sent by Cedrina. Being engulfed in feelings of appreciation for this transitional time of change left the guest a great deal to reflect upon during this particular afterglow of magical orange energy. This pleasurable atmosphere would keep the companions, for a time, in a cocoon of contentment in the little alcove space. Cedrina was certain that this euphoric feeling would last long into the day and deep into the night. She expressed appreciation with gratitude to the little glass water prism for its colourful reflective abilities. It was after all, a catalyst for the increase of superb memory awakenings.

The enchantment the guest felt during this morning's experience triggered a specific memory of a dream door that was once locked tight. Over the passage of time, with various life experiences that emerged in her life, this difficult door was determined to be connected with a deep, unhappy memory that created intense emotion whenever the memory surfaced. In the past, the door required a great deal of energy opening only one small inch at a time. In the dream, there was a blockage that appeared as thick, impenetrable vines requiring continued effort to remove in order to obtain free entrance. Over the last few years, this particular door was easier to open, at least far enough to get a glimpse of freedom from the disturbing memory. Each time she tried all remnants of uncomfortable emotion stemming from the deep turmoil that kept her feeling stuck in a dark place would dissipate a little more. This past memory reminded her of Cedrina's tale of the quest for freedom from the tiny winged creature trapped in the alcove. However, in this present moment, only a wide open door remained, requiring one to merely step across its threshold to a new world of freedom. How encouraging to find that such profound insights came merely by quieting one's mind and opening one's heart to the present moment. This amazing alertness to the open door brought surprise and amazement to the guest considering her past hesitancy of stepping through. This noticeable pause now seemed directly connected to finding the right time and place before being able to give full strength to her deep desire to be completely free from the anxiety-riddled experience. It was a most pleasurable outcome for the guest, because she was now able to bless the learning potential from the whole experience before releasing the dark memory with love.

Moment of Reflection

Orange: 'Sacral Chakra Relationships/Sexuality/ Empathy/Pleasure/well-being/connection, delight, emotions, feeling, polarity, change' (www.expressionsofspirit.com).

To Feel

In relationship to the chakra system, one can see the strong connection for needing to let go and the pleasure that comes from being able and willing to do so.

By releasing negativity that has been forgiven and perhaps even forgotten, emotional remnants often resurface into one's consciousness, creating the need to revisit in order to finally let go.

Truly letting go moves one through negative thoughts to one of submission, embracing what comes in one's life journey. The sacral chakra energy awareness experience brings much pleasure.

This specific colour energy brings to mind words of great wisdom.

'Many of our fears are tissue paper thin, and a single courageous step would carry us clear through them.' – Brendan Francis The Turmoil of Change

DAY OF SURPRISES

There was a lovely surprise happening for the companions. The Dear Ones had returned! It was late in the day when they both came bounding through the door just as the great light dipping past the horizon gave way to the beguiling half globe in the evening sky. A surge of love and appreciation washed over Cedrina for these special humans who played such a significant role in making dream- memory desires of a young red cedar come true. The Dear Ones were soon joined by the guest, and once they were all settled in the alcove, they proceeded to give an update to events regarding their time spent away from the homestead. It seemed that great changes would soon be taking place; they had made a decision to divide their time between residences in another country with a family member and the lakefront property high in the mountains. Many more household items would need to be sold, donated, or passed on to other family and friends. A few items would be taken to the lake property, leaving mainly personal belongings to follow them out of country. These dear humans went on to explain how difficult it was to let go of the many prized possessions that had become so dear to them over the years. They both had realized that for the necessary change to take place, no matter the difficulty of letting go, it had to be done.

A delightful surprise came when the Dear Ones offered an opportunity for their beloved visitor to choose from some favourite furniture pieces. They explained that it would bring them much pleasure and peace of mind knowing that a few of their treasures would be in safe keeping. The guest did not hesitate in choosing the little red cedar bench, the hat rack, and the mirror. Happy with the selection, the Dear Ones relayed that the only remaining dilemma was to find a good home for their tiny furry pet, to which the visitor eagerly replied, *'I would be more than willing to add her to the list.'* What a day for surprises!

Cedrina slipped eagerly into a quiet night of solitude, anticipating the interesting dream-memory whispers to follow. Due to the morning's exciting energy experience, the stage was now set for unusual memories coming out of nowhere. The first memory was the most unusual, considering the pleasure-filled experiences of the day. Uneasy stories that had been captured and carried by the strong winds of the past began to surface. During this memory time, the cedar tree was well accustomed to absorbing news from beyond the mountains. Awareness from this particular dream centred on restless, uneasy energy materializing from the distance as dense swirls of fog slowly crept closer. What was being relayed by the preceding breezes was not considered welcoming news.

It turned out to be a tale of great heat with high, angry flames from the other side of the mountain. There was, however, assurance that all was safe in the immediate surroundings in spite of the unnatural haze, which turned out to be drifting layers of smoke that slowly made their way over the mountains and across the lake. The winds began to howl as they relayed information from the devastating effects of the angry flames devouring many of the trees and helpless life-forms caught in the middle with no means of escape or rescue. Regretfully, those caught in the density of heat, flames, and smoke would dissolve, never to be heard from again. News of this type of dissipating life energy weighed heavily on all the energy life-forms in the lake area. They were left trembling in fear for what could be their own unwanted and unexpected fates.

It was well understood from past sharing messages that this hot, angry energy could be the result of great bolts of light made up of intense electrifying energy from high in the atmosphere above. Although destructive, it was considered part of a natural forest cycle of life that made way for new growth. Periodically, tales had been shared of similar forest damage known to have been caused by the unpredictable humans, who were often careless with their small campfires that they used to cook. During the time of this dream memory, the young cedar had never experienced such heat or had ever been exposed to the kind of flames that could do so much damage. The cedar wondered whether having a burning desire, such as the one she held so deep in her core to connect with humans, could possibly be similar to such a scorching as what was happening over the mountain on the other side of the lake.

DREAM WHISPERS OF
HUMAN CONNECTION

Exciting energy dreams quickly arose from the whispered news arriving with gentler breezes, providing much to speculate about for the little cedar. This new information was more welcomed, and it increased understanding as to what was happening nearby. These particular messages were deemed as 'reality pure', with little exaggeration, especially as wind whispers were from a collective movement of moving air that gathered information from ongoing connections of the sounds, smells, and energy from all in its path. What was gathered was considered a sacred duty that could not to be doubted by any forest energy life-forms. The cedar recalled one early spring when reality pure news arrived of humans setting up camp close to the lake's surroundings. This whispered news was most encouraging, bringing renewed hope that her dreams of human connection could indeed become a reality. The opportunity for human companionship would bring much joy and satisfaction to the young tree. The cedar again became aware of the warm sensation that triggered her burning desire for connection that had never left. Now, the wind had spoken, and things were definitely looking up.

Before too long, human contact messages were verified by many new arrivals to the area, such as the four-legged creatures exploring while in search of a safer haven to settle. They felt excited and anxious about the changes that soon would be taking place with the arrival of humans. Awareness of the necessity of reviewing options and perhaps migrating to denser forest areas free from human habitation was the predominant topic at that time. The alternative was locating safer places in the surrounding lake area that would be, for the most part, hidden from these two-legged humans that would surely come. The choice of description for humans as two legs seemed very appropriate, considering the humans were the larger of the free-moving creatures that they understood moved about on two legs.

In spite of the news, a variety of smaller creatures from the forest decided to stay put. They were noted as being very good at hiding and accustomed to having to move quickly to avoid detection. The winged creatures would have no trouble finding refuge among the thick branches, particularly those who were well settled in the boughs of the little cedar and other habitats nearby. Most of the winged creatures indicated they would not be leaving unless the humans decided to cut down the trees where they found shelter. It was thought by the forest life-forms to be a most peculiar habit of the two-legs, – their tenacity of eliminating well-established nesting sites. For some unfathomable reason, it seemed a most unnatural but common human activity that involved clearing out the thick forest brush and thinning out the trees and bushes. The two-legs were even spotted moving large rocks from the areas of their chosen campsites. Unfortunately for some of the forest life, this clearing process meant cutting down old and young trees, disrupting well-established habitats of many that sheltered in the area. However, some wildlife felt quite comfortable staying in such close proximity of humans because they knew of many species that had experienced a tolerable life among them.

Anticipation for the onset of humans ran high, with growing tales of interesting contact with the two-legs. There were the stories of extended generosity to some of the little creatures sharing space and experience with them. It seemed that many humans found much enjoyment in observing the little creatures. The little cedar paid eager attention these joyful stories and learned that some two-legs were even known to leave delicious gifts of unusual nourishment. It was also well understood that the two-legged humans could be quite crafty, often using this generous method as an incentive to lure the curious ones out of hiding. Extra care was called for regarding the natural urge to explore anything new, because it could have both good and unpleasant outcomes.

According to some brave little creatures, with the human invasion came great opportunities to explore, especially the structures left behind as the humans were known to leave the camp area before the deep sleep of winter arrived. It seemed that an abundance of interesting leftovers from the two-legs could be retrieved, making it well worth investigating for possible nourishment and nesting materials.

All the forest creatures that had decided to stay agreed that of course there was a need for great caution, because there were also horrific tales indicating great harm that could befall them if they became too friendly. It had been well understood that setting very nasty traps were also a common activity of humans in order to catch unsuspecting creatures for unfathomable reasons. Keeping out of sight whenever possible as well as treading carefully around the two-legs were understood as prophetic advice that should be taken very seriously. Without a doubt, it was the best line of defence against such unpredictable human creatures, who were attracted to these parts of the lake and forest.

It was an exciting time for the young red cedar, filled with high anticipation of human connection possibilities. It was easy to become lost in a dream world filled with speculation. The young tree was sure that it would be spared from being cleared away, because it was not yet grand enough for the service that her ancient ancestors had offered. How disappointing if the little cedar was to be discarded with no chance of fulfilling her dream destiny. At this time of her growth cycle, all the cedar could hope for was to bring abundant pleasure with her presence as a beautiful maturing specimen of a strong and healthy young tree. The cedar wanted desperately to absorb as much human energy as possible, and in order to do so, it must have an opportunity of closeness to the humans. This meant her growing position, sitting near a ridge that was close to the water's edge, was fortunate. She was found to be on a forest floor layer in a spot elevated enough to avoid damage from the high tides of spring water rising. It was the kind of location where humans liked to set up camp in order to watch nature in action and enjoy all that the lake could provide. There was so much peace and serenity, as well as nourishment and recreational opportunities to be had at the lake within her view.

The young cedar considered the location a most ideal spot with the very best advantage point for watching nature, and at the same time, the location had the greatest opportunity to be noticed. Nature watching was a common activity of humans, and this mountain area was located at the basin of the lake, with ample marsh area in view before the lake's waters moved on to become a small river. Energy forms made up of lake, river, marsh, and forest creatures in these surroundings provided great opportunities to experience nature in a most scenic, natural setting. Perhaps the humans would receive as much pleasure as the young cedar by watching the life cycles of abundant forest life found at this end of the little lake. Humans had the advantage with their ability to freely move about, and due to the building sites on a small hill; they could view nature from so many different angles. The little cedar decided she need not worry too much, because her location was the perfect spot for any humans who held an appreciation for nature. As far as the young cedar was concerned, grand times of living and experiencing both worlds were about to begin!

RAINY DAY BONDING

Over the next few days, heavy clouds shut out most of the great light, leaving the alcove with a pensive, quiet atmosphere. Great lapses of time passed with no signs of the Dear Ones, the guest, or even Furry Four Legs. The bench and hat rack missed the gatherings with their companions. After all, the life energy combination brought special, enjoyable energy to the alcove, creating a great deal of new understanding and adventure for them both. Not to be discouraged, Cedrina and the hat rack decided to take advantage of the quiet solitude, with only the rhythmic sound of raindrops against the window panes to keep them company. It would be an opportune time to reflect on long past forest lake surroundings, and perhaps some light could be shed on their mysterious past connection.

A surge of energy from the outdoors triggered a familiar atmosphere of forest living awareness. It seemed that the rain and wind wanted to join them, trying to penetrate the solitude of the alcove space. Waves of raindrops, from soft pitter-patter to heavy beatings, lashed against the window, adding to the depth of reflective energy that filled the atmosphere in the alcove. These sounds brought back a sense of closeness that the bench and hat rack experienced after the rather fortunate falling incident. Cedrina was now able to fill in some of the gaps of life in the forest for the hat rack through her dream- memories, bringing sharing awareness up to the transformation into her present form. Cedrina went on to explain to the rack, her experience tale during the time of her cedar tree energy becoming accustomed to the particular humans who shared the forest's lake location.

When the humans first arrived on the site, the majority of their time and physical energy was spent in preparation for their future use, by clearing the area to best meet human comfort and enjoyment. Every time the humans came near the little cedar, a bond of attachment deepened. Fortunately for the young cedar, the humans found in the midst of clearing her surroundings held much regard for all aspects of nature found within their campsite and the surrounding area. A new look to the forest lake area emerged, with the removal of many of the old and dying trees, the thick underbrush, and a smaller group of trees nearby. The humans made a clearing for them to settle on the highest layer, just as had been expected. Strangely, all the changes that took place brought a new element of natural beauty that provided a new vista for young cedar tree. These changes did not seem to interfere much with the peaceful solitude of the surroundings, and they actually added to the tranquillity and harmony experienced by anyone who dropped by for a visit.

The young cedar and the remaining little creatures quickly adapted to the new look and energy in the vicinity whenever the humans were present. There were a group of humans who were neighbours to the young tree's dear humans, who shared a large parcel of the lake front property. While preparing the forest area, they could be observed by the cedar helping each other, and they would often gather to relay how things were progressing. When they joined together, they shared nourishment while discussing ideas of how to improve their individual sites in order to maintain a 'back to nature' retreat for friends and family. Putting their combined ideas to work very often created loud, strange, and new sounds echoing throughout the surrounding forest, which were a bit disquieting for the little creatures in the area. It was a busy time for the humans as they went about building cabins and spaces to accommodate belongings that would make for comfortable living and sleeping during their visits to the area.

These humans arrived when days started to lengthen and the cool air was replaced with soothing, warm breezes brought in by gentle waves of energy coming from the great light. A bit later, at the season of longer days filled with light and heat, more human clusters arrived. As the seasons progressed, they would stay for longer and longer periods of time. During those warm days, sounds of human activity could be heard from both sides of the lake. Sometimes it was difficult to identify where the sounds were coming from; they echoed throughout the area, bouncing back and forth across the little lake surrounded by mountains.

During these times of human occupation within the immediate surroundings, the peace and quiet of early morning magically turned into a buzz of activity, creating a new, exciting atmosphere filled with unfathomable life energy sounds and aromas. This unusual commotion created quite a stir with the forest life, especially as the humans went about clearing and rearranging the natural habitat. There would often be a short quiet spell followed by a different sound and energy from the humans that emerged just as the great light would begin sinking behind the mountains. The pounding and buzzing atmosphere of daylight was replaced with a softer, vibrational murmur of human energy as they formed gatherings to share stories around a pit of flames, which sometimes lasted long into the night.

It was at these gatherings that sometimes a build-up of exuberance emerged from the humans sitting around the fire-pit. These meetings would often trigger an unsettling atmosphere of a need for caution with forest energy life-forms sharing the space. More caution was needed when the humans partook of a special mixture that seemed to bring out a different type of human energy, intensifying and heightening the energy during the gathering experience. It had been just such a time, when spirits were running high, that an unpredictable and bizarre occurrence took place.

Recalling once again the unusual time and space of this unpredictable event, Cedrina fell deeper into the dream as she relived the experience as the young red cedar tree. She had found that prior to this high-spirited campfire gathering, the atmosphere thickened and became heavy, as if materializing out of nowhere, just like a dark cloud about to descend on the life energies of anyone in the immediate area. The young cedar recalled that there had been a deep core instinct warning that night, indicating an extraordinary event was about to take place. This event would bring with it unusual sensations that penetrated her core being and outer tree layer – a prelude to a tremendous transformation that would eventually take place and change the cedar's tree energy form and natural life span forever. How uncanny that this very night's strange experience would become the catalyst for eventually fulfilling the cedar's great desire for a closer connection to the humans.

Preceding the life-changing event, the young tree found it most intriguing to observe human responsiveness to each other, going through levels of excessive highs and lows, depending on how many humans were settled around the pit of flames. There was one very distinctive human presence, a visitor in the area, who was especially notable, giving off abundant dark, moody energy. This human previously displayed difficulty in adjusting to the quiet solitude of the area, and by the evening he seemed altogether out of place, as well as out of sorts, with the rest of the group. The visitor was staying as a guest at the same campsite of the young cedar's dear humans. It seemed the visitor shared a very strong energy connection and bond with them. What was most notable about the energy of this visiting guest was his display of nervous and unpredictable actions, which were accompanied by an intense vibration of deep brooding. It was this anxious energy that made him stand out from all the other humans. Even the young cedar viewed him as extremely unpredictable simply because he would spend much time in a state of anxiety–riddled reflection that soon turned into agitation. These actions were a far cry from the peaceful and insightful energy displayed by others at the campsite. Caution warnings whispered throughout the whole area whenever he was observed.

It soon became evident that the restlessness exhibited from this particular human would often be taken out on the surrounding forest life. Some of the trees nearby would receive a swift kick whenever he passed by them. The receiving tree life energy considered it a most unusual mode of making connection. With each kick, a shock of agitated energy penetrated the particular tree, which in turn would absorb a sensation of deep sadness for the individual. Not surprising, the little creatures went into hiding whenever this human approached, because they sensed his dark, fearful energy. This display of frustration, of what could only be described as fear energy, escalated as the anxiety riddled guest began throwing stones at any creature in sight. He also went down by the peaceful shoreline of the little lake, throwing rocks and stones at winged creatures and water creatures alike. The only break for forest life would come when his extraordinarily anxious energy became restrained whenever one of the other humans approached. These humans offered calming comfort to the troubled human whenever possible. Indeed, it was noted by all who crossed this human's path that they were dealing with a very tortured energy being. After he gave apologies, agitation soon resumed, and before long most of the humans in the area did their best to avoid connecting to the hopelessness exuding from this human. The only remaining semblance of loyalty, strained as it was, came from the cedar's Dear Ones.

The young cedar found it most peculiar that this human guest rejected the peace and tranquillity of the area. If anyone needed the soothing relief of what was offered through nature, it was this troubled human who exhibited so much turmoil and pain. Perhaps it was the reason for his invitation in the first place. This particular human was soon known to all of nature's life-forms in the vicinity as the 'Anxious One,' and because this human was in the habit of displaying such odd behaviour and refusing the healing energy so readily available, it was best for all forest creatures to keep a wide berth. Nature's forest life had never been as quiet as when the Anxious One was up and about; the normally peaceful campfire gathering was no exception because the humans too would become quiet when he arrived.

TROUBLED GATHERING

When it was time to gather at the pit of fire, the humans often added a strange, strong-smelling liquid that created huge flames. Putrid, dark smoke rose from the fire-pit and spread throughout the open area. Strange as it was, this foul odour and thick smoke would soon give way to a slow and gentle flame that brought much pleasure to the merrymaking humans. The strange liquid was kept near the fire in a brightly coloured container for easy access. Whenever this fluid was used, care and attention was given to where the liquid landed. It seemed on this particular evening that a greater amount of anxious energy was felt by all who gathered around the fire-pit. An increase of uneasiness hung heavy in the air when the Anxious One insisted on being the one to start the fire. It was during the preparation for the flames that the Anxious One became agitated because there was very little liquid left in the container. An unexpected gesture as a result of his agitation startled everyone: he threw the container into the nearby trees.

The container hit against the young cedar before landing with a resounding thud at the root base, spilling some of the strange-smelling liquid down her trunk. The cedar tree remembered a strange, tingling sensation as the liquid coated the outer layer before being quickly absorbed into the deep crevices of her bark. She was accustomed to strange liquids being sprayed, because some life-forms would dampen her base. However, the cedar tree did not find those experiences to exude as foul of an odour as the liquid presently soaking past her protective cover. She wondered how long it would be before the odour dissipated.

All went quiet around the pit of fire for a moment or two, but relief came when someone arrived at the site with a full container. Gaiety could again resume, albeit a bit more subdued, from the normal cheerfulness of past gatherings. As the fire quickly started, the throwing action was not so easily forgotten by the hosting Dear Ones, whose complete astonishment at such a dangerous gesture quickly turned to deep anger. They directed harsh words at the Anxious One, who at that time, held a long stick that was ablaze. Without a moment's notice, he jumped to his feet, shouting that no real harm was done. He threw the fire stick at the young, liquid-soaked cedar. The others gave great gasps of disbelief as they watched in horror. A burst of flames quickly sprang up on the young tree. The gesture sent everyone into complete shock as they tried to make sense of how such a careless action could have taken place. Had it not been for the quick action of one of the humans near the tree, who knows what could have happened? This quick-thinking human was able to put out the flames with a cover the humans had brought with them to keep out the late night's chill. This quick action from the mindful human would be thought of as no less than a miracle by a hero who saved the day.

UNUSUAL
ADAPTATIONS

CEDAR TREE ALTERATION

The once pristine outer protection layer of cedar bark was now compromised, leaving the tree with a great black scar. The young cedar was as much surprised at what took place as the rest of the fire-pit company. A great sigh of relief was heard throughout the little group at being rescued from the possibility of a most horrendous outcome. It was difficult for them to comprehend such a careless action that put everyone in harm's way. This would be a hard night to forget, even for the forest life-forms that had witnessed such dangerous and destructive energy from the anxiety-riddled human. Many awareness tales would be passed on by the humans about this night – and most assuredly by the young cedar, because she would certainly share this peculiar experience with other energy life-forms in the vicinity. The young tree was beginning to understand the unpredictability of humans, as suggested by the tales from other creatures that had witnessed that very same strange human energy.

The Anxious One, a most troubled guest, was very contrite about what had taken place, and he felt it necessary to leave first thing the next morning. A great sigh of relief was heard through the forest the day of his leaving. Later that same day, the atmosphere returned to the accustomed sights and sounds of peaceful forest lake energy and pleasant observation of human activity.

Over the passing of many seasons, the anxiety of the incident was put aside, and life with the humans returned to a cycle of campsite work, rest, and gaiety. Over time, visits from the Dear Ones were scarcer, although neighbours would sometimes make a point to stop by and examine the gradually expanding gaping scar on the young tree. As the cedar grew, so did the scarred patch of missing bark. The young cedar was unable to hold onto her outer bark from the blackened area as it slowly disintegrated and fell away, especially during the winter months. It seemed that the cedar would be forever scarred, with a portion of inner red cedar grain partially exposed. The outer layer had been loosened, and tiny creatures would attempt to burrow into the delicate wood, although few were actually successful due to the natural red cedar repellent. Still, some of the little critters were beginning to make progress. For the most part, the repellent was able to keep them from burrowing in too deep, thus saving the tree from greater damage.

Even if the damage was not life-threatening, the gaping scar would, over time, have a devastating effect on the young cedar's life span. Left with most strange sensations with each invasion of tiny creatures, the young cedar now had to come to terms with new awareness energy of irritation. Thankfully, this irritable, itchy sensation was often followed by the tapping sound of a winged creature coming to the rescue, finding nourishment from the tiny creatures, relieving the itch and thus saving the core of the young cedar.

An unusual consequence of having such a scar was a seasonal visit from a couple of large, furry dark creatures known as black bears to the humans that were able to put the prickly area to good use. The scar was now easily spotted by the big creatures once the young cedar had grown in height, density, and girth. The cedar tree had matured to a strong, sturdy red cedar, and she was now able to withstand the tough pressure of the bulky creatures. It seemed they found the scar area just bristly enough to rub against, and the spot was capable of relieving some irritable discomfort of their own. In the end, the predicaments of irritability of both energy life-forms became very satisfied with the scratching post service. A mutually pleasurable experience was actually set in motion by the growing scar.

Unfortunately, this pleasure did not extend to the burrowing attempts of the tiny creatures, temporarily sabotaged during this scratching post ritual. How extraordinary that such a close call of destruction to the young cedar could reach such a mutually satisfying conclusion, adding to the cedar's list of rendered services, especially for the life-forms found in the area.

REMINDER OF
CEDAR ENERGY

As Cedrina shared these dream-memories with the hat rack, a new appreciation developed between the two. They both now could better understand the life energy of a red cedar tree. In present form, the bench, although considerably smaller in stature, continued to hold strong cedar life awareness to core memories. Cedrina also held a certain fascination and gratitude to her Dear Ones for making use of so much of her life-form material, turning it into a serviceable object by putting to good use the special repellent hidden in her core. As a cedar bench, Cedrina very much appreciated that she could still be a means of cedar protection for items safely stored away, and at the same time, she was able to display the beauty of her natural red grain. Life energy as a cedar, even in the form of a bench, maintained the commission of providing safe sanctuary, keeping with the red cedar's tradition and purpose. The added bonus was in providing precious service to her dear humans as the ideal place to sit and relax, giving opportunity of continual loving contact.

The hat rack was taller in stature maintaining a tree-life form providing service with its curved, outstretched arms as the ideal resting place for the Dear Ones' hats and scarves. Not to be forgotten, it remained a constant reminder to cedar tree existence. The base of the hat rack did stretch out in four directions, leaving an impression of above-ground roots, which were a common feature of older cedar trees. Unfortunately, the hat rack was completely covered by paint and was still unable to exhibit any real beauty and warmth of red cedar grain, as did the little bench. Although, the gap from the damage caused in the falling incident with Furry Four Legs could be considered an exception. Cedrina was pleased with the now visible scar on the hat rack. This fact alone brought about a rise in status, a reminder of the unusual experiences when she also carried a gaping scar from the ordeal with the anxious human long ago. Time had indeed served them well in fulfilling the past dream quest of service to humans, at least as far as the little bench was concerned. Cedrina very much appreciated the joint connection to share some forest tree awareness memories.

In spite of having the pleasure of connection with the hat rack, Cedrina felt a most peculiar sense that something was missing. The awareness connection that had just taken place during these past days filled with moments of sharing, left an even deeper core cavity that needed to be filled; there continued to be a few blanks, and Cedrina hoped that perhaps the hat rack could soon provide a few more clues. Could there possibly be an even stronger connection between the two? The little bench was fairly certain they came from the same forest area. When all was said and done, there were dream-memories yet to be unveiled. Cedrina instinctively sensed that the hat rack too was able to maintain faded memories that could perhaps shed some light on her deep-seeded curiosity. How could she know that very soon it would be the hat rack that would play a significant role in unravelling the mystery? Questions that had engulfed them both during their transformation in form would soon be answered.

Moment of Reflection

It seems not all that uncommon for the deep turmoil and anxiety that is often found in the life energy of humans, specifically those related to deep-seeded frustrations, are easily taken out on others, or at the very least, on things that offer little resistance if only to be used as a point of release.

Perhaps the real challenge for humans is in getting a grip on the overspill of this type of energy anger outlet capable of creating such unpredictable, dangerous behaviours.

Could it be that other energy life-forms such as trees are capable of awareness and sensitivity to the anxiety of humans?

As awareness and connection to nature grows, so too will human care and compassion, taking greater care of all life-forms that share in our world of energy experiences.

UNDER A SPELL

ENERGY GIFT OF STRENGTH – TO WILL

As anticipated, the water prism again worked magic with the arrival of early morning rays, reflecting a most astonishing, bright, golden yellow glow throughout the alcove space. Just coming out from dream state, Cedrina was surprised and confused with the power and intensity of this awakening light. She found it to be as bright as the great light's penetrating rays shining through clear skies over the forest lake at midday. This was the most powerful light energy time in those past days of forest life. For a brief moment, she found it difficult to distinguish whether the cedar's core energy was a tree, located in the deep forest absorbing the strength from the great light, or here in the alcove in her present form of a bench. Could she really be sitting in a rural country home in an alcove space recalling awareness of a past light energy? There was no end to this amazing glow as it entered the space and continued a magical journey bouncing off the mirror and sending rays back through the window to the great outdoors.

In this delightful moment of light, Cedrina experienced ecstasy in a reflective mist of past tree life memories, with Mother Earth bringing awareness of nourishment to her energy core. As awareness grew, she was able to sense some kind of movement taking place between two strong energies, from the great light above and from Mother Earth below. The combinations of these two powerful energies triggered a profound sense of peace and contentment throughout her cedar core. It seemed that even within the core consciousness of the cedar bench, this mysterious experience of two energies collided. This collision only reinforced Cedrina's deep-seeded desire, intention, and determination for sharing her life energy story. For Cedrina, this golden energy experience created a valuable space of awareness of extraordinary will and power buried deep within her energy life-form.

The experience of such power was a new sensation for Cedrina, extinguishing all doubts of the future and dissipating any nagging remnants of insecurity into tiny particles of dust. As these dust particles dissipated, her past doubts became lighter, gently floating away just as dream-memory whispers brought a flood of reminiscence from past tranquil moments by the lake. Golden awakening memory whispers soon arrived in the form of fast-moving lake water rushing in and overflowing the banks, bringing bits of recollections as gifts from the lake, waiting to be explored. A groundbreaking recollection was about to burst into the peace and contentment that Cedrina and the hat rack experienced. Both now found themselves back in a dream-memory of the forest energy from whence they came.

Human Enchantment

Many growth seasons had passed since the dreadful incident from the burning liquid. In spite of the scar – a reminder of human frustration – the cedar retained deep core intuition that all would be fine with the humans returning to the area each summer season. The young cedar eagerly anticipated the numerous opportunities to observe human interaction at the campsite, especially when they sat around the fire-pit. It was as if a spell would forever surround the young cedar tree, and she became totally engrossed with gleeful human energy that filtered through the wisps of smoke and snapping sparks rising up from the flames. Laughter and deep discussion filled the air with abundant human liveliness as they once again relaxed together around a glowing fire, enjoying the night sounds of nature in such a tranquil atmosphere.

Huge pits of fire were a common sight along the banks of both sides of the lake and it seemed to all the surrounding forest energy, an enjoyable pastime for humans in the area. Depending on the breezes, varying degrees of sounds drifted into the warm, dark nights, filling the air with intriguing sounds coming from instruments played by the humans gathered around the flames. To the young cedar, those sounds were just as sweet as birds singing and calling to each other, encouraging tranquil admiration and attention. At times the harmonious sounds of human voices cast a spell of pleasure, keeping time with the soft, vibrational energy from the strumming of the instrument and producing moments of pure delight for the young cedar.

As usual, the young cedar found during the daylight hours, the campsites were abuzz with human activity as they busily went about improving the area for even greater pleasure and delight. And oh, what grand enjoyment was observed from all that the little lake could offer. Many of the campers seemed to find great satisfaction in exerting themselves in a most energetic activity, splashing about in the water. Sometimes loud and noisy devices that skimmed the water's surface were used by the humans, creating an abundance of joy. On other occasions, smaller, quiet craft could be observed silently gliding across the surface, with soft, smooth, rhythmic sounds of paddling motions keeping the serenity of the lake intact.

This slow and quiet gliding brought back memories of the young cedar's awareness of envy for life-forms that could easily move with the flow, especially while observing floating tree trunks moving with the water's current. These currents would often carry them to the high reeds at the end of the lake. On a few occasions, the logs would wash up on the shoreline along the way. No matter the landing, the logs always brought news and excitement to many curious life-forms in the area. There were even times when a human would climb on a log for a ride, as did some of the winged creatures found in the area. It was common practice for the winged creatures to hop on a floating log and go for a glide down the lake. It seemed that both humans and the winged ones had something in common after all.

There was an interesting recollection that surfaced for Cedrina of one human enjoying a leisurely ride, slowly paddling across the lake with a large winged one spotted sitting at the opposite end of the log. It seemed they both enjoyed the peace and solitude of a smooth, pleasant ride. This sight was all the more endearing due to a mutual understanding that during times of water play, humans and the wildlife did not really mix together. All of the water creatures tried to keep a good distance from the unpredictable humans at play. The flying winged creatures, not content to share the lake during those exuberant noisy times, usually made themselves scarce. It was very odd indeed to observe these two different species enjoying the lake's quiet solitude together in such close proximity, let alone sharing the very same log. Both energy life-forms must surely have been under a very deep spell of enchantment.

FOREST CLEARING

Forest clearing in the area continued each warm season, with the cutting away of old, dying trees and the removal of heavy forest brush – seen by many humans as unsightly – at least in the areas where they set up camp. Oddly enough, the human element did not hold the same sentiment about life as other forest life energies regarding the importance and purpose of the declining life cycle of fallen trees. It was difficult to understand how humans viewed old, dead trees as eyesores and a hindrance that needed to be removed and designated for an altogether different purpose. Much of the wood from the dead, dying trees were cut into smaller pieces and used as fuel for the fire-pits.

The young red cedar often wondered about this human practice of cutting old trees for making fires. Perhaps it was similar to what took place in the awareness tales told by the old, dying tree from the past relaying to her as a young curious and impressionable cedar about the great ancestors that enjoyed human contact. If so, how marvellous it must be for these old ones to be experiencing firsthand such a unique service for humans at the end of their tree life cycles.

The young cedar at that time, was happy that her old friend from the past had long ago dissipated back into Mother Earth, leaving very little as a reminder of having existed at all. It would have been very difficult for the old one to have been cleared away without having the chance to fulfil its own decaying destiny as a tree log capable of conveying its cedar history to the nearby saplings. The wisdom from the old, dying tree would continue as long as the young cedar was persistent with taking opportunities to connect and share with any new saplings sprouting nearby. The cedar knew without a doubt that at least a few saplings would survive and continue the tradition. How could they not? After all – it was the proud red cedar tradition!

The young cedar had to admit that she missed the tree life energies that were removed, especially the friendly birch tree that had been so helpful in her early maturing stages of life. Recalling the past connection with the young birch, the cedar found 'widow maker' as a declared nickname for birch trees by some humans – very odd. Understanding soon surfaced after a particularly bad storm, when the friendly birch was found splintered right down the middle of its core and fell with a resounding crash to the forest floor. Soon thereafter, once the humans arrived, the splintered birch ended up being one of the trees that were removed.

It had been during the removal of her birch tree friend that the young cedar overheard a discussion on the reasoning behind the strange birch designation of widow maker. It seemed the unusual name came from old tales that had been passed down among human tree cutters from the past. The name was chosen due to a common trait of the birch tree to easily fall to the forest floor. It seemed the life core energy of the birch was more rigid and often unable to bend with the high winds that often flared up during heavy storms. The fragile trees would sometimes crack deep into their core and become weak, frequently crashing down at the most inopportune moments when humans were present. Many times the trees would fall on those who happened to be clearing brush nearby. Depending on the size of the tree, a falling incident could easily result in fatal consequences. Cedrina was well aware of humans having mates just as other energy life-forms, and when she considered that losing one in such a manner would be most unpleasant, perhaps it was not such a strange name after all.

The soil in the forest lake area was very fertile, and the humans would take advantage of the richness by transplanting plants and bushes, and strange as it was, sometimes even large rocks. Humans seemed to hold an attraction to the dense energy coming from hefty rocks. They would move them about their campsites from time to time along with large pieces of driftwood that washed up on the shore of the little lake. The rocks and driftwood would be precisely placed to add the human perception of natural beauty. Those who shared the sites spent a great deal of time and care with any changes made in the surrounding landscape or building that took place, all the while making sure the end result was a congenial fit with the natural environment. For quite some time now, the young cedar was able to enjoy fleeting connection moments with her dear humans, sensing a great depth of appreciation for nature evidenced by her with all the care and attention given to her immediate surroundings.

It had not gone unnoticed by the young cedar that one of the dear humans liked creating new items out of the natural wood collected from the forest area. Much of what he created came from what was salvageable from the forest cuttings that took place. Of course he also used supplies that he'd brought with him to the site. The young cedar recognized unfamiliar long boards of wood that were sometimes hauled in by the humans' vehicles. To the smaller forest creatures, these hauling vehicles were seen as 'unpredictable, moving noise makers' squishing anything in their path. The noise alone from these vehicles created quite a stir, sending creatures scampering for cover in all directions to get away from the commotion that followed. It was not uncommon for humans from nearby campsites to gather and unload what was hauled in to the site. Curiosity and helpfulness were common traits of the humans who shared space in this area.

The young cedar watched in awe as a large shelter being built by the Dear Ones took shape. The building was called a cookhouse by them and had included a very impressive deck attached. The cookhouse location had a tremendously good viewing advantage, being built on the higher third level tier of a small hill overlooking the shoreline. It held a tremendous view of the second lower tier where the fire-pit was located. As an observation point, it was viewed by the cedar as perfect, especially as the fire-pit was very close to the young tree. The spot chosen for the deck had a bird's-eye view of lake, nearby marsh, fire-pit and best of all, the magnificent, young red cedar tree.

Lovely aromas and uplifting energy followed the dear humans as they went about turning the site into a lovely garden filled with nature's natural beauty. The serenity of the space that they were able to achieve was admired by many in the area. A Dear One would often be observed creating both small and large items before disappearing with his handiwork into the newly built building. Where the newly made items ended up was a mystery to the cedar. Just as the tree's surrounding area had gone through a human created transition, it seemed that the young cedar was soon to go through an even greater one.

TIME OF TRANSFORMATION

APPROACHING CHANGE

The forest lake dream-memory whispers continued, as did the flow of golden light weaving a heavy cloak of intense awareness to her past tree life energy for Cedrina. As a young cedar tree, she was always thrilled with any contact opportunity with her Dear Ones, especially when they came to examine the length and depth of her scar. With each connection moment, Cedrina sensed anxious energy of great concern for her. As time passed, she found each and every contact contained a strong, loving vibration, providing the young tree with an exhilarating hope for continuous connection. It was during one of those intense bonding moments that the young tree picked up deep remorse coming from one of her dear humans.

The young cedar quickly sensed a deep feeling of regret from the Dear One that seemed to be tied to the incident responsible for creating the now gaping scar along her trunk. It was so long ago and so much had happened in the area since that distant past event. The wound on the tree had long healed over through numerous growing seasons, which brought strength and expansion to the life force of the young cedar. The tree continued to thrive in spite of the growing scar that was becoming larger and rougher with each passing year. This escalation of scar expansion was mostly due to the bears using it as a scratching post. On this particular visit it had been determined by the Dear One that the open scar area was fast becoming more vulnerable – not just from the rough treatment from the bears, but also with the harshness of winter and heavy weather storms that popped up from time to time. Especially worrisome was the increase of tiny little creatures slowly making headway with numerous attempts to burrow into the young cedar's very inner core. Concerned with what was happening, the Dear One made a decision to bring down the tree before the damage worsened.

Sincere deliberation took place over the finality of this decision, especially because the tree was still considered by many of the campers as very healthy. As far as many of them were concerned, the tree had numerous good years ahead before the inevitability of removal would need to take place. Some humans were strongly opposed to this solution, feeling that things should be left as natural as possible, at least as long as the tree's situation did not became too unsightly. For them, the young tree provided a perfect observation point for them to get an excellent glimpse of the black bears arriving for a springtime scratching session.

No matter the opposition, since the young cedar was found on the property site of the Dear One it remained subject to his choice. The young cedar would eventually need to succumb to a different fate than popular opinion. Not wanting to leave the young tree's survival up to the elements, he determined that in the very near future, the time had come for the removal of his favourite tree.

Another growing season had passed since the last loving connection between the cedar and her dear humans. This time however, the human contact was very different. What could now be happening? The cedar was suddenly aware of peculiar, indescribable vibrations penetrating through her very core. Following these vibrations, the tree had a most unusual sensation of being separated from limbs and roots, followed by moments made up of traumatic periods of darkness. There were now disquieting moments of intense vibration where the young cedar became completely disoriented as her outer layer was removed. Her delicate inner wood core was sliced and cut into long, separate pieces.

In the middle of the disorientation taking place, the Dear One whistled a happy tune, oblivious to the turmoil taking place within the deep core of cedar tree energy. In spite of everything, unfathomable calmness descended upon the red cedar core and began to take a strong hold. Along with the merry tunes, there emerged a new awareness of sincere, kind, and caring energy never before experienced from the Dear One that travelled straight to her inner core as she lay askew and scattered in so many separate pieces.

The sensations experienced during this separation ordeal differed greatly from what was previously understood about the change of form through the tales of the ancients, as told by the old, dying tree. Or was it really? How strange to find that, no longer in tree form, the cedar continued in awareness of life's energy. The young tree had previously understood that such a change in form would be the end of all desire, intention, or speculation about what future cycles would bring. The awareness tales passed down and shared from past cedars were thought to be ended with the alteration in form by the ancient peoples. There were no continuing tales passed on after a change in form took place, indicating energy awareness had stopped with the transformation. The young cedar thought it should have been the end of awareness after being cut away from one's root system.

What would become of her as she went through this strange conversion into another form? As the branches fell away, the young cedar found that important sensor connections were broken, and she could only hope that some of her seeds cradled within the branches would fall and take hold, to be cradled in the nourishing earth and eventually blossoming into new life. Tiny particles of wood dust flew everywhere as the steady burr of the saw cut deep into the cedar's life core. There now remained only a small hope that as the wood dust settled, it too would sink deep into the ground, fulfilling a small portion of tree destiny by returning to Mother Earth.

While being cut, shaved, pounded, and made into completely different shapes by the gentle hands of the

Dear One, the young tree was able to review all of her life experiences in flashes. A strange, euphoric sensation to this change emerged during a sanding that brought out the beauty of her natural grain. This euphoric sensation remained in spite of fully understanding that all her previous desires for the future in tree energy form would no longer be attainable. The cedar would not reach her predestined height in order to view the greater surrounding area, and neither would she be a part of the magnificence of her surrounding environment. Providing nourishment for other life energies in the wonderful forest lake location was no longer possible. Most peculiar of all during this disconcerting time was coming to awareness that her cedar energy could still be alert to that of contentment. It was truly amazing that after all that had happened, life energy continued even with this new, unique change in appearance. A realization soon began to sink in that a new purpose also followed the change in form.

How peculiar that the last memory to surface for Cedrina during this golden, light energy moment was observing what looked to be a long pole made from the young cedar material as it was being transformed into a separate object. Astonishment arose within Cedrina, with this new awareness that the object had a distinct designation as that of a hat rack. The dream-memory whisper was now complete; a mystery was now solved with this vision of awareness. The two separate objects were placed together as a newly created red cedar bench and a freshly made cedar hat rack. This newly formed insight of being united brought amazement to both the little bench and hat rack. With heightened pleasure, they both were able to understand they were not only similar in past tree energy – they were designated as hand-crafted creations of the Dear One, and they came from the very same cedar tree!

It was during this dream-memory that Cedrina again observed the Dear One as he stepped back to admire his creations. With a broad grin of satisfaction, he pronounced the duo Latin names: Rubeo Cedrina, meaning 'little red cedar'. No longer in tree form and separated in purpose, there was a distinct impression that Cedrina the little bench and Rubeo the hat rack, were actually created to be together as a pair. This premise was assured because the Dear One took the time to carve Latin words, 'Heri Foveat – Cras Somnnia – Vivere Hodie', on the backrest of the little cedar bench, and then the English translation, 'Cherish Yesterday – Dream Tomorrow – Live Today' on the base block piece just over the legs of the hat rack. It had been deemed by the Dear One as the most excellent means of distinguishing the duo forever entwined as a set. How extraordinary that this new, profound information in thought and deed had taken place so long ago and only came to the surface at this moment in time. How could such an event have ever been forgotten by Cedrina or Rubeo? What could have happened to separate the twosome for so long? Deep in the core memory, an understanding began to surface that there was yet more connection awareness to surface.

Return to Golden Light

Focus returned to the alcove with the arrival of the guest who, unable to suppress a gasp of pure astonishment as she stepped into golden light, took a deep breath to fill her lungs with golden energy. Feeling suddenly inspired and filled with delight for the moment, she swooped up Furry Four Legs and whispered, '*Oh, what enchantment I have stepped into.*' She slowly made a full-circle twirl in the doorway. After softly dropping the furry creature to the floor, the guest then stood firmly on the ground with her arms raised high into the air. She began to twirl around in circles in the middle of the golden glow that surrounded her. A truly magical moment was in full swing as feelings and sensation of oneness emerged. Her arms started overhead and then slowly moved in a downwards arc while she twirled in the middle of the room. The guest created an alluring vortex, drawing in the other companions' energies.

As the energies combined, it was difficult to distinguish where each energy glow began and ended. Enmeshed as one at that specific moment of time, new awareness to life force energy that affects and connects every living thing on the planet she felt took place with the four companions. This exceptional understanding added strength to the overall connection experience that was happening with this glorious, golden light. Becoming one in purpose, one in connection, and one in communicating deep-seeded commitment intentions to each other was the outcome.

It was now just as important to the guest as it was to Rubeo, the hat rack and Cedrina, the cedar bench to express understanding, knowledge, and wisdom gained from life journey experiences. The intentions to stay connected and share the entire story of the separation that took place so long ago took precedence for the hat rack. Rubeo was now fully aware that a door of expression had opened to a more broadened understanding of an essential part of the young red cedar story. Loyalty and desires for continued connection, close to the guest from this time forward was guaranteed by Furry Four Legs. The opportunity to remain together thrilled this group of companions. It did not matter how long the magical connection would last; the life energy of each was forever changed, and there was no turning back from such a bonded connection.

The guest lost no time in putting the story to paper, finding that with each passing moment, she felt immersed in a powerful force of love, and she was deeply motivated to reveal what took place. It was a very unusual occurrence to put to words. Writing about this particular golden energy reflection while feeling the intensity of the companion connection as one, and yet still individual energies within the group, would indeed be a challenge to explain. She also came to a conclusion regarding the importance placed on expressing separateness. Each of the companions held unique life energy experiences, and each held the desire to share awareness stories; all were of equal importance. There was yet more to be revealed from this unusual gathering of individual life force energies.

Moment of Reflection

Yellow: *'Solar Plexus Chakra stimulating Will/Power/Joy/ Motivation self-esteem transformation, vitality, energy standing steady in your own self, desire to express individuality' (www. expressionsofspirit.com).*

To Will

This powerful, golden yellow energy brings awareness to a feeling of being uplifted, with a deep desire to draw strength from others as a teamwork effort.

The team linking, as reflected with the unique connection that took place between the four companions, brings to mind words relating to a most extraordinary work of healing.

> *I choose to live through the open space in my heart as I search out love and appreciation for all that surrounds me no matter where my journey leads.*

> Louise L. Hay

It is believed that those words speak for all of life connections, whether spoken from a physical heart and mind, or from silent core life energy.

The search for love, appreciation, and understanding is observable in all life-forms throughout the planet. We need only open our hearts to unique life force possibility.

ENERGY GIFT OF THE HEART – TO LOVE

The promise of a lovely sun-filled day arrived with the first rays of light that reached deep within the alcove space. Awakening from deep dream sleep, Cedrina and Rubeo were found entwined by spirit and surrounded in a sea of emerald green. Today's prism gift penetrated deep into core energy, bringing a sensation of love and expansion. This expanding energy was sensed as a flowing movement, stepping over a threshold into the presence of something divine. Deep awareness soon followed to the relationship of past growth experiences and the fresh spring promise of new budding life that took place in the early spring surroundings of the young cedar tree. A truly blissful awakening experience was about to begin from a dream-memory whisper with this deep colour of emerald green.

It was strange that after having many previous recollections from memory whispers, this dream returned again to an earlier time of young cedar tree energy. It seemed that the sea of green energy was a reminder of the wisdom from the birch tree coming to fulfilment for the little cedar so diligently following growth instructions. It had been that very reaching – high towards the light and deep down into Mother Earth – that resulted in growth, maturity and strength, and it did indeed set in motion freedom from overwhelming fear. The young sapling learned to let go and give in to the steady growth taking place every growing season. Slowly but surely, the little cedar would rise in height and expand in width, resulting in a strong, healthy young red cedar. This new acceleration of tree expansion each growing season, along with the steady cycle of budding seeds taking place from branches, were found to be in perfect balance. With growth came new experiences, and with new experience came more knowledge.

A constant flow of interesting information arrived with visitors to the cedar's strong, healthy, outstretched branches, which easily transferred what was gathered to her inner core. The cedar's location also added to growing interest and consideration from many forest creature visitors that stopped by to rest amongst her fast-growing branches. Because of her ideal location, a time came when tree dimension and size was no longer an issue that discouraged connection. In spite of the close proximity of much larger and taller trees – all excellent sources of sanctuary and nourishment outweighing the little cedar – she did enjoy a high degree of vigorous growth, encouraging interesting and unusual awareness connections. It seemed that connections by the other forest life-forms improved, as did the area view of the young cedar's surroundings. This new attention was thanks to the clearing of heavy brush and older dying trees by the humans. The young cedar's branches were now strong enough to offer a perfect place of refuge for any life-forms that took full advantage of all that the young tree could offer.

The young cedar branches quickly became a haven for an abundance of winged creatures both large and small, turning the tree to a hub of socialization. The large juvenile winged creatures, coming from a nest farther up the lake, often sat on the very top of the cedar because they could now enjoy the exceptional view of the lake and patiently wait for their favourite food to appear as they swam close to the lake's surface. Many adventure stories were shared as each partook of connection opportunities whenever the younger great ones dropped by for a visit.

A variety of smaller winged creatures were often found within the strong, thick branches that provided more protection from seasonal storms and the gusty winds of winter. The branches of the young cedar were now considered a perfect sanctuary to bring new life, and they were abuzz with all the nesting taking place in the growing seasons of spring and early summer. Whispered dream-memories made up of pleasant chattering and fresh sounds of new life brought great contentment and a fulfilment of purpose to the young tree. Appreciating this abundant ongoing service kept the young tree busy, and she forgot completely the limitations of her early sapling days.

News and information arrived from varying directions as the cedar branches transferred what could be learned from each of the vantage points they faced. The expanding trunk brought ongoing life awareness from the world perspective of smaller creatures, some winged and some crawling, in search of nourishment and protection. New tiny lodgers took advantage of hiding places under the loosened bark and the inner exposed fragile portion of the young tree, just as the wise, old, dying tree had explained so long ago. No matter the circumstances or minor annoyance felt by this invasion, the young cedar was happy to provide sanctuary service. As far as the little cedar could surmise, spirit energy and matter were in perfect balance. As a red cedar, core energy was filled to capacity with appreciation for the magical green haven offered to all the creatures partaking of her steadily growing energy.

LOVE ENERGY EXPANDING

The guest soon arrived at the alcove during the last few moments of the all-encompassing vibrancy of emerald green energy. Once again a feeling of stepping into an atmosphere of tranquil love and comfort took hold. She felt a swelling of the heart while breathing in the loving energy of this wonderful, velvety-rich colour. Strong intuition surfaced for the guest, now standing in the middle of the little alcove with her hand over her heart. She repeated words of appreciation for all energy gifts received at this special moment in time. *'My heart beats to the rhythm of love.'* Cedrina and Rubeo both experienced great waves of the loving energy encompassing them all. While basking in this love energy, the guest took tender care to prepare the companions for what was soon to take place with upcoming travel plans.

It seemed they would be leaving as soon as arrangements for transportation could be made. Although the trip would be long and arduous, the mirror, bench, and hat rack would be bundled together and enclosed in a van. Furry Four Legs would travel in a carrying cage, riding up front with the guest. Because the trip was in early summer, there was a good chance for perfect travelling weather. Taking in this new plan, both Cedrina and Rubeo slowly emerged into the past with a travelling experience from a dream–memory that held untold excitement with energy connections made during the journey. This journey took place shortly after the life–form transformation.

Amazing memories bubbled to the surface. First awareness opened with a vision of being loaded on the back of a truck, where for the very first time, they experience forward movement. This movement was heightened with the sensation of being in the middle of a circling wind while travelling. The journey began on a bright, sunny day with nothing but blue skies overhead. Travelling on such a clear day enabled Rubeo and Cedrina to witness new and unusual life energy sights and sounds flashing by on the mountain roads. While travelling through the mountains, they were provided with the most interesting panoramic view of life energy that seemed to pass by so quickly. Although unable to share connections with the endless profusion of life energy swirling by, they both became acutely aware of passing through a never–ending, magnificent forest.

It was this fast-moving sea of green whizzing by that astonished both Rubeo and Cedrina, so much that any uneasiness with the unknown future dissipated in the swirling air. Moving through such a profusion of energy with the encircling wind provided an eerie impression of moving through a hazy fog. It was a very strange and glorious sensation in comparison to what was left behind when standing still and attached to the forest floor in the middle of an enveloping morning mist. It was so exhilarating to imagine all the future connections that were bound to take place, giving the opportunity to share this amazing journey story.

EXPLORING NEW HORIZONS

The Journey Adventure Story Unfolds

Not long into the travel journey, while still being hemmed in with trees on all sides, an interesting energy experience took place at a point where the vehicle slowed almost to a stop. Slowly sauntering across the path of the truck was a large black bear with two small cubs nearby. Rubeo and Cedrina immediately became aware of the familiar energy, sensing tree life once again where one of her branches could have reached out and caressed the thick black fur as they passed. Rubeo was very sensitive to this memory and strongly sensed the familiarity of the creatures close up and personal; the passing bears were the very same creatures that made such good use of the young cedar as a convenient scratching post. It was with this memory that the hat rack felt a small, tingling vibration in a particular scar area still visible on its pole. It was as if the bears had come to connect one more time to give a farewell to the young cedar life energy that they had come to appreciate on their early spring route.

A few stops were made along the journey, allowing a much-needed break for the Dear One driving, along with a reprieve from the fast, whirling movement of surrounding winds that were part of the journey for Rubeo and Cedrina. These stops provided the bench and hat rack a new, different view while observing humans tumbling out of vehicles to stretch their legs. Sometimes these humans paused for a moment to admire the surrounding scenery before disappearing into the larger building. Most thrilling was when the human passersby caught a glimpse of the duo and came to admire the freshly handcrafted cedar forms sitting so proudly in back of the open truck. There seemed to be a great deal of human comings and goings at each of the stops made along the way.

At one of the stops, a memorable connection took place with a small, four-legged creature hanging out of a vehicle that had pulled up beside them. With its head sticking out, a short connection was possible. The bench was amazed that this little creature resembled one of the rocks, called Dog's Head Rock that was part of the lake area property that they had just left. A slight awareness of loss quickly entered the core of Cedrina, giving a pang of regret at knowing the environment of the past was no longer part of this new life energy. This regret only lasted a moment because the little creature managed to captivate Cedrina and Rubeo with a journey tale shared with its humans, heading to a campsite high in the mountains.

Having visited the site before as an important human travelling companion, the little creature was looking forward to the sights and sounds of the forest campsite. As a pet of the humans, it was well aware that the journey experience would be filled with opportunities to explore an abundance of life energy creatures within the campsite surroundings. The little creature could hardly contain its growing excitement that the site was getting closer, sensing a familiar energy to the immediate surroundings. What great pleasures would be had, chasing and exploring many new and enticing places, sights, and sounds while in the company of its wonderful human masters. If any danger lurked nearby, it would keep them safe by announcing it very loudly.

This knowledge being shared came as no real surprise to Cedrina; she was well aware that protection and safety seemed to be the natural intention and purpose of these four-legged human companions. A protection purpose was demonstrated by a similar pet life-form that accompanied the Dear Ones at the lake. Strangely enough, size did not enter into the equation because both large and small pets seemed capable of scaring off much larger, wild, four-legged creatures if they dared come near while their humans were in the vicinity. This little four-legged creature was no exception, emitting a loyal and joyful attachment that was very evident with the return of its humans. Its attention was diverted as the humans neared the excited pet. The small creature was now totally engulfed in re-establishing connection, jumping with glee and eagerly devouring small treats that surfaced in the reunion. The awareness connection for the little bench and hat rack dissipated as the happy group drove away.

Soon the Dear Ones returned to the truck, and the journey was resumed. It was time again to be mesmerized with the strange moving sensation. While on the roadway, many vehicles passed them by just like the wind, too fast to make any kind of connection. Some stayed directly behind for a good while before eventually passing, providing moments to take in the varying sounds coming from the vehicles. A couple of times the vehicles on the move would make strange honking sounds, triggering a whispered memory of life energy from the sound vibration coming from a flock of winged creatures, named by humans as geese, as they flew over the lake near the cedar tree. Nostalgic awareness resurfaced with recollections of numerous adventures and connections of past days. With each memory came a realization that the wonderful lake area would soon become a misty memory of the past.

ANCIENT FOREST CONNECTION

Cedrina and Rubeo soon recalled the most sensational awareness and connection experience from this transitional journey. It had taken place at the last stop, made just before leaving the mountain region. This memory was especially poignant because the sights and sounds were again relived in memory. A tremendous vibrational pull to a particular area filled with ancient red cedars took a strong hold deep in the cedar core of both. During this stop, they had memories of all the wisdom passed down from the cedar's old friend, the dying tree. Memories and stories from the past that had been shared, and so much more, came flooding through like a tidal wave.

This wonderful spot was known as the Red Cedar Forest. The forest held so many vibrations calling out, so powerful and intense, that awareness connection took immediate hold, requiring little linking effort on the part of Rubeo or Cedrina. Awareness was quickly established with untold numbers of old and dying trees, young and new saplings, and various life energy varieties of foliage that resided in this special place. A gentle breeze added to the nostalgic connection taking place, filling deep-seeded appreciation for the wonders of this old-growth forest. Untold new information added to previous ancestral dream-memories, providing in-depth understanding to cedar destiny as a sanctuary and nourishment to other forest energy life-forms.

Rubeo and Cedrina learned how the hollow cores of large, old-growth cedars were used for winter dens by black bears similar to the ones from the forest lake area. Cedrina and Rubeo had wondered where the dens were located at the little lake area, and they mused over similar possibilities. It had been impossible to know where the creatures that visited the lake site came from, because dens would have been hidden deeper into the forest and a good distance from any humans in the area. The twosome learned that woodchips from the scraping out of the den would be used as bedding for the creatures, bringing new life into the world while still residing in the winter dens. The large trees nearest to the den would be used to keep the young creatures safe because they climbed high in the trees if threatened.

Cedrina and Rubeo went into an immediate recall from the life as a cedar tree, witnessing and experiencing three little creatures climbing high in the trees near the lake on the command of the larger one. These little ones did not climb back down until they were given the all-clear. How wonderful it must be for the great trees in this area to be such an important sanctuary for these interesting creatures. What joy it must have been to explore the natural surroundings of cedars and play and rest in branches. It was a great place to catch early spring warm rays from the light.

Amongst the sharing connections that surfaced during this special forest visit was awareness of a new life energy form, described as having four long and lanky legs that moved very quickly. The humans called them caribou. These creatures would find nourishment in this forest in the early winter before heading up to the higher regions of the mountains. They would make use of old growth rainforests, feeding on the abundance of shrubs that were sheltered from early season snowfall by the thick cedar and hemlock canopies. These lovely creatures would return again in the spring to take advantage of the abundance of sweet, new growth.

Cedrina was again reminded how upright, decaying trees stayed intact for many years, providing habitation for many life-forms such as cavity-nesting birds and mammals. The age of the trees from this forest were considered very ancient; many of the trees were over five hundred years old. It was understood that the longevity of the trees in this ancient place were the result of moist, westerly air flows from a large body of water (the Pacific Ocean) rising over the mountains. Cedrina was in awe of the joy that must have come to this forest as these westerly winds arrived, bringing with them a continuous flow of amazing tales and knowledge from afar. How wonderful it must be to be located in such an area and to have experienced the growing seasons of this unique forest with incredible amounts of rain and snow that would have created so many unusual life energy connections. The combination of spring snowmelt followed by abundant rainfall during the growing seasons alone made it a perfect, lush forest environment, where varieties of life-forms were found in abundance.

New knowledge was indeed gleaned from this visit. It was truly a magical place filled with many of the young cedar's ancestors – the only place where such a rainforest existed so far away from an ocean coastline. It was difficult to express the magnificence of these mighty cedars found in the old forest. Nothing of the sort in height or girth could be observed in the forest lake left behind. The information gathered from this majestic place triggered a deeper appreciation for being part of such a noble ancestry for Cedrina and Rubeo, even if it was only for a short time in tree energy form.

THE ADVENTURE
CONTINUES

The duo was temporarily lured into the magic and wonder of the ancient cedar tree enchantment, and they did not realize they had resumed their journey. They recalled being pulled back to a present moment of travelling by a violent jerk as the vehicle came to a sudden stop. Something had happened farther up the road, causing traffic to come to a complete halt. They had been so deep into memories, lulled by the steady drone of tires and the whistling of the wind during travel, that they had lost immediate surrounding awareness altogether. The vehicle soon resumed its movement, albeit noticeably slower.

Cedrina and Rubeo quickly connected with what had created the strong tug that shook them from the old forest enchantment. There had been a collision between a smaller vehicle and a large, four-legged, antlered creature that had tried to cross the vehicle's path. While slowly passing the scene, Cedrina picked up a faint energy vibration just as the life energy of the creature left its physical form. She was able to observe the fading energy as it drifted joyfully into the atmosphere, back to its source. Life energy in spirit for this creature would be forever changed. The unusual incident was deemed very sacred by both Cedrina and Rubeo, who were in awe at having been able to witness such a magnificent transformation. Great cedar tree curiosity engulfed the duo as they wondered what types of sensations would have been experienced by the creature during its separation from life energy. Would it be a similar experience as with the young cedar's transformational experience? Could the lifeless life-form now lying by the side of the road continue in service, providing nourishment to other life-forms while dissipating back to Mother Earth? Perhaps one day in some far distant future, the twosome would also experience a similar, final transition back to source. At least at this point, curiosity for both Cedrina and Rubeo was still intact.

As the speed of travel picked up, Cedrina became aware of a change of familiar tree energy. The region being observed was now much flatter, replacing the familiar dense forest area. Upon sensing this change, Cedrina tried to stay focused on being grateful for being with the Dear Ones, with all the opportunities for continued human contact, and with the interesting sharing prospects that would surely follow. Imagination and curiosity soared, as did the surrounding air movement within the strangeness of sights and sounds of the new, open spaces passing by.

Before too long, the travelling duo entered into a higher density of human energy filled with many human dwellings lined up close together. For some strange reason, this new vibration became irritating to Cedrina. So much of what they now experienced indicated to the little bench and the hat rack that they were out of place in these new surroundings. Cedrina was perplexed by the depth of uneasiness she experienced with this new energy, which now filled the atmosphere. It was different compared to the peace and tranquillity of her forest dwelling left far behind. Nagging doubts soon surfaced, leaving her with an unusual sense of foreboding that took hold while she moved through this strange, unknown territory.

JOURNEY'S LAST STOP

It seemed there was one more stop before reaching the final rural home destination. This last stop was where Cedrina quickly became engulfed with incredible shock that left the bench totally distressed. Something as close and familiar as a part of her cedar energy was again being taken away. The past uncomfortable sensation again surfaced, much like when branches of the young cedar were cut away and discarded. A very deep void took hold as the hat rack was gently lifted up, only to be removed from Cedrina's side and taken into a building where all connection was lost. How strange that up until this very moment, this memory and sense of impending emptiness had been completely lost to Cedrina.

Returning to the here and now moment of the little alcove, both Rubeo and Cedrina marvelled at the intensity of this particular dream whisper. They wondered how such a memory could have been so profoundly veiled for so long. It was especially fascinating to Cedrina that such a strong vibrational pull of energy from the old-growth forest could have been buried so deeply from her awareness. The loss to this journey adventure memory could only be compared as a dense forest fog that was so heavy it completely blanketed the thick undergrowth of the forest floor from where they'd originated. The fog could only be removed by the strong rays of the great light, which would dissipate its density. Incredibly, it took the same kind of strong emerald rays to release this hidden memory of separation.

While reliving this travel journey, especially with the old forest vibrational experience, a powerful sense of belonging and purpose arose in both Rubeo and Cedrina, who now had a strong awareness to the bonding connection that would dwell with them for a long time to come. No matter what the future held, it would now be accepted with deep, overflowing appreciation for the amazing, opportune moments of exploration and sharing. It was at this moment that the companions concluded that life was what one made of it!

The guest was astonished as she looked again at the chakra connection with the enchanting life energy between the companions gathered in the alcove. If there was anything one could count on, it would have to be a natural, emerging intuition taking place with these extraordinary and unusual experiences. The guest was able to formulate an intuitive affirmation that seemed to fit so completely. *'I release the past and am free to move forward with love in my heart and core, completely trusting in the process of life.'*

While eagerly writing all that she learned from the gathered information of today's experience, the guest recognised that this shared journey story was more than one of mere connection. It was also a tale of deep harmony and fulfilment of purpose. How wonderful that Rubeo and Cedrina were able to be reunited after being separate for so long. It would be interesting to hear the details of the missing pieces, which would need to come from Rubeo in order to complete the red cedar's life story.

Moment of Reflection

Green: 'Heart Chakra stimulates Compassion/Love/open-hearted desire for self-acceptance, balance emotions, harmony, place of integration' (www.expressionsofspirit.com).

To Love

While pondering on a human life experience, especially with a separation and transitional loss situation, it would seem that there remains a need and willingness to accept what has taken place in order to find balance and peace of mind.

Accepting whatever the future brings often holds the key to a sense of happiness and joy from all that can be learned from any experience. With this expectation comes awareness that a joyous life really is subject to self-love and acceptance.

One could say that it takes a heart and mind expansion to all connections of life moving one to awareness that all life is connected and deserving of harmonious existence in a world of change.

Loving the self in order to love all life seems a profound key to happiness.

UNLOCKING MYSTERIES

THE TALE OF FURRY FOUR LEGS

The following early sunrise was well hidden behind large grey clouds that left a steady drizzle of rain in its place. A mid-morning gathering would not be deterred, taking place in any case. In this moment in time on such a damp, drizzly day, all energy life-forms in the household felt drawn to the charm of the alcove, making it the cosiest place to be.

The first to arrive was the guest, and she snuggled up in the blue shawl that provided her warmth and comfort as protection from the cool, damp morning air. Trailing close behind was Furry Four Legs, quickly settling in to begin a purring regime. It seemed the perfect kind of morning to hear endearing tales of love and courage that warmed the heart and brought solace to the mind. A notable spike in warm energy to the little space was felt as soon as the Dear Ones arrived, bringing with them a tray of the warm, sweet-smelling beverage that added to an atmosphere of such charming surroundings. Before finding a comfy spot on the deep window ledge, one of the Dear Ones stopped to gently pat Furry Four Legs. Endearing attention was brought to the tiny ball of fur upon hearing the statement that the creature would be greatly missed once they went their separate ways. This cosy atmosphere spurred the guest on to inquire when the little cat first became a part of this cheerful household. The Dear Ones related the story of Tiny, their chosen name for this furry creature.

Before they began the tale, the guest felt inclined to share how a strong bond with the tiny ball of fur had surfaced when she'd first arrived. What was most intriguing about this special relationship was a fast-developing empathy tied to a moment of the reflective thought process that would arise whenever they got together in the alcove. This unusual occurrence would take place just as Tiny would start its purring ritual. The guest went on to explain her conviction that enthusiastic purring and thought-provoking words were somehow linked to early sunrises. The best way she could describe it was as morning ritual occurrences that set in motion seemingly magical moments of profound, meditative experiences.

This morning's reflective consideration was made up of these words. *'I am grateful to be alive, and what pleasure it is to live yet another splendid day.'* The words seemed to materialize from the vibration of the little ball of fur, taking on a mantra quality. It was as if the tiny cat set the tone for what was about to take place in each of the profound morning experiences. Because of the ongoing ritualistic sequence of events that routinely followed, there was a deep, heartfelt feeling that this strange, furry creature had chosen this particular household as a place to belong – hence the guest's inquiry about from whence this wonderful creature had come.

The Dear Ones were pleased to fill in the arrival details of Tiny. They started the homecoming tale by first explaining about an ongoing occurrence that often took place in these rural surroundings, with city folks discarding unwanted pets. They went on to explain that many small animals were dropped off on country roads. Unfortunately, due to the wildlife in the area and the need to cross over many fields and ditches before finding shelter, not too many of the abandoned creatures survived.

As it turned out, this particular tiny one had a tremendous will to live, and for unfathomable reasons it was thought to have been on some kind of mission to come to this particular family. There were a couple household properties between the common drop-off point, where the bedraggled creature would have had opportunity to find shelter and nourishment. Many fine people in the surrounding area demonstrated compassion for any of the unwanted pets that managed to survive. This kindness was especially true for the neighbours just across the road, who were known to take in any strays that made it this far. Their farm and acreage seemed to be a beacon as a sanctuary for stragglers. However, for some unfathomable reason,

Tiny ignored the beacon and picked this household as its chosen destination.

The Dear Ones explained that on the day of Tiny's arrival to their home, two years back, it had been a damp and rainy morning very similar to the present. The first inkling of what was to take place started with their pet dog, Tessa, becoming unusually restless, running back and forth from the alcove to the kitchen and trying desperately to get their attention. The Dear Ones were stunned by such unusual antics demonstrated by the old girl, who managed to eventually capture their attention. Tessa persistently jumped on and off the little cedar bench, making a strange sound with her barking that they'd never before heard. The barking sounded almost like words – 'Look, now. Look!' All the while she was peering intently through the alcove window. Upon investigating what the fuss was about, they observed a tiny, wretched, rain-soaked creature slowly making its way up the driveway, only to collapse at the bottom of the front steps.

At first they thought it was a small rat because of the scrawny body. After checking it out, they soon realized that it was another drop-off, and they immediately brought the tiny one indoors to examine it. It quickly became apparent that the prognosis for survival was not good, however as soon as they picked it up, they felt a vibration that enticed them to take extra care. They both immediately felt that because the tiny thing had made it this far, it deserved the best care available. They were not disinclined to taking in strays, and they determined that this bedraggled creature was meant to be here. The tiny one was close to expiring, and so a trip to the vet became the order of the day.

They thought that it was just a young kitten, and so they were very surprised when the vet explained it was at least a two year old. Based on its physical condition, it had gone through a very difficult journey on its way to their door. Its heart was weak, and the vet determined that getting stronger would depend on its own will to survive. The little creature would need a great deal of tender loving care even for a fifty-fifty chance of survival. There were obvious signs of injury, more than likely occurring from a life-threatening confrontation that likely would have taken place after being dropped off. The tiny thing showed the after-effects from one or more fights that resulted in a few partially healed body scars, a gash over one eye, and most noticeably a large nick out of one ear. With care, the wounds would completely heal, however it would likely be left with a slight limp from a badly damaged hind leg.

The Dear Ones decided to nurse the wee thing back to health, and they quickly became quite fond of what turned out to be a white and ashen small ball of fluff. The tiny creature demonstrated a regal, independent disposition that quickly became evident once healing had taken place. With this fact in mind, they thought about calling it Princess, however because of its small size, the name Tiny seemed more appropriate.

The unique independence of Tiny became apparent during the first few weeks, and it established its place as if it had always been a part of the household. It was only a matter of days, after rising from its sick bed, before the tiny creature did a disappearing act, retreating into the lower level of the home. They felt that because it had gone through such an ordeal, perhaps it was better to let the furry creature have as much solitude as it wanted. After a time, they would only be able to catch a glimpse of the animal early in the morning and at evening feeding time.

The Dear Ones explained that when Tiny did appear at feeding time, it would accept little attention from them, and any established connection or affection seemed, at least at that time, to be with their pet dog, Tessa. They also thought it very strange that it was only during early sunrise that Tiny would be found curled up on a napping blanket in the corner of the kitchen beside the dog. To add to the mystery surrounding this little furry creature, they could detect a loud purring throughout the house when Tiny was nowhere to be seen. They thought such a volume of purring produced from such a tiny creature was very unusual. In spite of a quick recovery, this strange cat remained small in size.

The odd behaviour continued well past the period of adjustment, up until the Dear Ones were faced with a personal tragedy. It was during a poignant moment of deep sadness when attachment changes with Tiny actually took place. A new, closer attachment was eventually established and took on the connection pattern in the form of the pleasant ritual in the alcove each mid-morning. Their pet dog was very happy and contented with this change in attention, and now she once again could stretch out on her blanket with no interruption. This new pattern continued until recent times with the arrival of the guest, indicating that an obvious, gentle shift in loyalty and attachment had indeed taken place.

Tiny had the unique ability to quickly bring calmness to any kind of upsetting situation. The example related by the Dear Ones was the anxious time when they had just received upsetting news of the passing of a loved one. Strangely, this loved one who had passed turned out to be the Anxious One. This dear friend of theirs had been the one who received Rubeo, the hat rack, as a gift. It was during this difficult grieving time that Tiny gave unusual attentive signs of connection to them. This attachment became evident with a tiny ball of fur pacing back and forth, rubbing up against their legs and purring loudly.

The day of the phone call, as they sat around the dining room table in shock from the news, Tiny jumped up onto the table – something it had never done before or ever again – and proceeded to gently lick their hands, which were covering faces streaked with tears of grief. When they moved their hands down, Tiny softly pawed their faces, and the volume of purring became louder.

Since that day, a much stronger bond took hold, and the little furry creature began to join them in the alcove. Tiny would quietly follow them as they made their way to the special spot atop the little bench, and they had quiet moments of peace and solitude. The Dear Ones had the distinct suspicion that Tiny was keeping a close eye on them.

PURRING EFFECTS

The Dear Ones continued with their tale by explaining that during one of those cosy alcove moments, they realised the depth of appreciation they felt for the magnificent purring that came from their tiny pet. It seemed that as soon as Tiny settled on the bench and snuggled between them, the purring ritual began. Before long they came to awareness with the sound and vibration of purring and a strong, direct link to the intensity of their feelings. If they were feeling uneasy or upset, the purring became so incredibly loud that they could feel a vibration resonating throughout the room. Every time this type of purring took place, calmness washed over weary nerves like a waterfall bringing refreshing, cool water to a stagnant pool. When all was well in the household, the purring was very quiet and smooth, like soft ripples in a pond creating a pleasant, enchanting atmosphere and enabling deeper relaxation, sometimes even making it difficult to leave the room.

An unusual aspect that surfaced about Furry Four Legs during this tale was its gift of healing as well as its ability to soothe. The Dear Ones explained that they had firsthand knowledge of a healing quality during times of personal stress. They also recalled an unusual purring time when their beloved pet dog, Tessa, had come down with a serious heart and breathing ailment. So serious was her ailment that Tessa had to be rushed to the vet. The vet indicated that the illness would not go away; the dog was very old, and there was little hope of recovery. The vet recommended they put the little dog out of her misery, believing it would be the best for all concerned because the condition would only worsen – and very quickly.

The Dear Ones, being much attached to their pet, said they would think it over, but for the moment they were not ready for such a final act. They brought her back home instead. They knew it would be a few days until they could came to terms with what seemed like the only option for relief for their dear pet. Immediately upon their return, Tiny curled up against the little dog and began purring loudly. The strong vibration once again could be heard throughout the whole house. It did not matter which room in the house they entered; the loud purring followed as if it was right beside them. The old, weak, and weary little dog did not seem to mind, and so the Dear Ones left them in peace.

It took two days before a noticeable change took place. During those two days, the little ball of fur would not leave the dog's side, even refusing nourishment. It was hard to comprehend where the strength was coming from without any food or drink to sustain what would surely be required by such a tiny creature. On the second day, Tessa rose from her sick bed and immediately went to her feeding dish. This was the first time the little dog had shown any interest in eating since becoming ill. By the end of the day, the dog was asking to go outside, and after one more night with her faithful sleeping companion, she showed absolutely no signs of the illness. Strange as this was, she seemed perkier than before. Things quickly turned back to normal, with Tiny once again joining them in the alcove, leaving Tessa to leisurely stretch out in her corner retreat in the kitchen.

On the fourth day, they returned with the dog to the vet, and to the astonishment of them all, Tessa came home with a clean bill of health. Even the vet could not believe that such a miracle could have taken place. For some unexplainable reason, Tessa showed the signs of a much younger dog. The vet indicated that Tessa seemed to have the health and stamina of a dog at least five years younger. This was so very surprising considering her state of health a week earlier. After learning of the sequence of events with the little cat, the vet relayed that she had heard of such powers of healing with this type of purring vibration. The vet explained the results of a study about that very thing. It turned out that cat purrs exist in a vibrational range with medical therapeutic potential. The explanation given to the unusual purring phenomena indicated that the average house cat's purr had a frequency between twenty-five and fifteen hertz – the same frequencies where muscles and bones were able to repair themselves. A theory was put into place that cats could be self-healing. Studies showed that vibrations at those frequencies could be beneficial to humans as well; these studies came from the *Fauna Communications Research Institute* and found that every single cat had purr vibrations well within the 'medically therapeutic' range (20–140 hertz).

The vet was pleased to experience the phenomenon firsthand and declared that she would give it more attention in her practice. This information would certainly explain the survival of Tiny and the purring that took place during those first healing days after arriving at her new home. The vet made a request to use Tiny as a means to do a study of her own, but the Dear Ones could not bring themselves to part with their tiny pet for the length of time that would be needed, and they respectfully declined.

It was at this point the Dear Ones indicated that giving up Tiny was not an easy task – understandable considering the uniqueness of the adorable creature. However, they decided that because of the unsettling changes that were about to take place, and after seeing the new attachment and mutual connection between the tiny cat and their guest, they were sure it was a good decision. They had no doubts that their little pet would be in loving, caring hands. The guest was ever so pleased with the amazing story of Furry Four Legs and the unique information supplied; it shed new light on the unusual bond that spoke to what was taking place with the powerful experiences in the confines of the alcove. The little ball of fur would be a most treasured companion.

Moments of Reflection

Perhaps the phenomenon of Furry Four Legs having therapeutic value holds true, considering it is well accepted that cats were admired in the past for their abilities to resist harm.

Studies show that the purring aspect of cats gives evidence of a unique ability to regenerate the body, and it is used as a therapeutic apparatus to speed recovery, which is observed when cats are wounded, frightened, or giving birth. This understanding expands the idea that cats only purr when content. Humans in the past not only worshipped cats but used similar vibratory methods, with the use of percussion instruments to induce healing.

Is it really so farfetched to have a connection between what is being described with Tiny and the guest, and vibrational healing with spoken mantras in the practice of meditation? Remarkably, the word 'mantra' is a Sanskrit word and translates to the phrase 'mind instrument' – much like a cat's purr. A great deal more on this phenomenon can be found from the article 'Cat Purrs Harness Holistic Healing Powers' (thespiritscience.net).

ENERGY GIFT OF
EXPRESSION – TO SPEAK

Sometime during the night, the rain finally came to a stop. With the early morning sky clear, the light rays that were soon to appear would be intense. Sure enough, it was at the first, precise moment of reflection through the little prism that an unbelievable, surreal atmosphere of deep blue filled the alcove space. Cedrina immediately remembered a past experience with this wonderful colour through a dream-memory whisper, becoming lost into the vast blueness of the sky. It was a perfect distraction from the strange sensations that were taking place within this dream, the time of tree separation from roots, and changes that were taking place before the creation of her present form. In the dream-memory, there were bizarre connections to Rubeo, standing nearby during that long-ago experience. Due to this particular dream, a new phase of awareness was about to take place in the present moment.

The purring from Furry Four Legs took on a whimsical, uplifting, vibrational sound, very much like a distant whisper penetrating through a thick, almost impenetrable mist from the past. The momentum of purring moved the close companions to an extraordinary awareness of being in a dimension where the air was pure and life energy seemed as light as a feather. This out–of–world experience would forever change the energy link between Rubeo and Cedrina. This link was so intense that dream–memory whispers from both the hat rack and little bench now presented as one, making it difficult to identify from where the memory was coming. This oneness experience brought to the surface a deep–seeded awareness of a strong urge of expression for Rubeo, who now found it easy to relate the missing piece of the unusual separation story.

The dream tale of Rubeo started with a recollection of standing tall and erect in the middle of an open, grassy space. The pole slowly came to awareness of being beside the newly made red cedar bench. The sky at that time of dream recollection was a beautiful deep blue, much like what was being experienced in the present atmosphere of the alcove space. It seemed that the magical gift of colour seeped into the energy core of the two, just as it once did when they stood separate but side by side in a completely different area of the forest lake site from whence they'd grown as a young cedar tree. Strange indeed, sensing three separate positions at the same time – the alcove, the location as a tree rooted in Mother Earth, and transformation to a completely different space in the middle of a field.

In spite of having been severed from its roots as a young cedar, there remained an unwavering sense that all was well, even with the drastic life energy change in form. In this campsite location where both separate life-forms stood, there was an awareness of the tree stump, still solidly rooted in the earth as a portion of the young cedar tree energy. There was no doubt that this cedar tree portion would continue providing sanctuary to the little creatures of the area. All of the past tree memories of what had been growing in the forest would remain, to be passed on in these surroundings as long as the cedar stump remained.

Separation from the stump soon created a huge gap in the core memory for Cedrina. During that transformation time, comprehension of life energy proved a bit awkward; she was no longer a whole, complete tree. It seemed that awareness came from all parts, each bringing energy and life perspectives, spilt in so many separate sections and leaving a huge void with cedar energy, which was no longer able to connect to the main cedar core. Life energy would remain in part with the cedar stump and root system, but it would be forever lost to the newly created forms of the bench and hat rack, as would the fast-depleting energy attached to the cedar's beautiful branches. It was so strange to know that part of one's life energy was still rooted, and yet to be completely unaware of what was happening in that state.

In this dream whisper, with the Dear One whistling his merry tune, the memory of the scar from the scorching event surfaced. At this moment of the dream, the hat rack was the one most able to tune into a portion of the scar memory, still apparent in spite of all the changes in form that had taken place. It seemed that the Dear One decided to leave a portion of the scar as a reminder of the seriousness of what had happened that dreadful night long ago. Who would have believed that the experience during such a distressing event could have such a long-reaching and profound impact on them all?

It was during this creative transformation that the newly made hat rack again sensed the close connection between the Dear One and the anxious human, who was the catalyst for all the changes taking place. The Dear One was taking great care, putting the final sanding touches over the scar area on the pole of the hat rack, when a most remarkable coincidence took place. An unexpected visit from his dear friend would bring with it yet another change, because it took place on the very same day the rack was receiving the final touches. Very pleased with the results of his creation, the Dear One proudly showed off his handiwork, making a point of showing to his friend the special words so carefully carved at the base of the rack. He carefully explained the origins of the newly made hat rack as the young cedar from the past, and he made it a point to include the reason for leaving part of the scar visible.

The friend, no longer filled with anxious energy, could hardly believe all that had taken place so long ago, and once again he apologized for what had happened.

He relayed that no matter what kind of anguish he had experienced at that dreadful time, there was no excuse for his horrendous lack of respect for others, or for his deplorable behaviour towards nature. It had been a very strange time for him that would not be easily forgotten. As difficult as it was, over time he found the courage to move forward with some semblance of dignity, and he took the necessary steps to straighten out his life. The friend implied great interest in the newly made hat rack, declaring that owning such an object would certainly serve as a constant reminder of the past, when they both had shared grand companionship while growing up together. He was especially interested in the special words carved so carefully at the base, declaring that they were wonderful words by which to live. The remaining visible scar on the pole of the rack would certainly be a reminder to stay calm and collected, restraining from any future 'over the top' emotional outbursts.

Hearing what his friend had to say moved the Dear One immensely, and in spite of his intended plan to keep the bench and hat rack together as a pair, he made the difficult decision to make Rubeo a gift of love for the past, present, and future happiness to his beloved friend and childhood companion. He declared that it would be dropped off on the journey back home later in the season, after closing camp. Appreciating such a grand gesture of love, the friend graciously accepted, stating the gift would be treasured for the remainder of his life.

True to his word, on the journey home, the Dear One lovingly carried the precious gift up a flight of stairs and set the rack down in the corner beside the passageway of his friend's front door. Rubeo recalled that time and was aware that before leaving, the Dear One did a final check by examining every detail of his creative endeavour, making sure it had not received any damage from the journey. Satisfied that all was well and anxious to get home before dark, the Dear One said his farewells, pausing just long enough to remind his friend that if at any time he felt the need to be rid of his belongings, the Dear One would appreciate having first dibs on the hat rack. The now grateful friend declared it would be highly unlikely, with all the changes he had made in his life. He could think of nothing that would induce the need to let go of such a valued gift. After sharing that, he fully understood the reason for the gift, as a reminder of past transgression, and he promised that if anything happened, Rubeo would indeed be returned.

LIFE CONNECTION WITH THE QUIET ONE

Although the space was dim with no natural light to bring warmth and vibrancy to such intriguing wood grain, Rubeo soon adjusted and became comfortable in a world of quiet solitude. In this quiet retreat, the rack settled with a few moments of joy filled delight, especially with the merry sound of whistling that came from his new owner as he went about daily chores. Rubeo identified him as the Quiet One, with very little contact made between the two. Over time, the hat rack became accustomed to the total silence and darkness of the surroundings, especially during the long span of time when the Quiet One was away from the premises. The only energy contact that Rubeo received was when this quiet human would pause to admire the rack on the way out, and he'd periodically stop and say, *'Thank you,'* while cautiously caressing the pole where a portion of the scar remained.

The verbal response and caress routine became a ritual over many seasons. This ritualistic connection continued until a profound moment, when another change in the atmosphere took place. It was this new transition that was responsible for the rack's coolness and blocking of any kind of life energy expression, making it impossible to connect with others. Uncomfortable awareness of agitation around the remaining scar area now resurfaced as Rubeo brought the rest of the companions up to date on the reason for the multiple layers of dark, glossy paint.

It had been a peculiar day that started with a delightful atmosphere filled with intriguing sounds of whistling and other merry tunes coming from the Quiet One. The Quiet One took extra care in wiping down the rack and lovingly caressing the intriguing words at the base, and he proceeded to wrap the pole with sparkly material that glistened and brightened the little hallway when the light was turned on. It seemed that a special time of celebration for humans had again arrived, only this time there seemed to be more intensity to life energy within the normally calm and quiet human. This energy connection was so rare, in fact, that Rubeo could not recall ever witnessing such a joyous occasion of awareness.

The Quiet One had left the premises in a light-hearted and jovial mood that somehow had gone through a complete transformation during his time away. Upon returning, there was no sign of the previous uplifting energy – only the sense of a deep, foreboding darkness that hung heavy in the air. What could be detected was very much like the early warnings of an oncoming storm filled with unfathomable darkness and intensity ready to burst. Unsure of his footing and balance, the now thunderous human stumbled through the door and came to a full stop, facing the hat rack. The lights turned on, and the now extremely agitated human intently glared at the rack's visible scar. Moments slowly passed, and without any warning, he kicked the base of the rack. Without a moment of hesitation, awareness of the Anxious One from long ago had returned in full force to Rubeo.

While relaying this part of the tale, Rubeo sank deeper into the event that took place during this thunderous attack. None of the previous gentle energy was noted by the rack at that time, because awareness was now totally focused on the anxiety-riddled one as he grasped the rack tightly, roughly picked it up, and threw it down the hall. Hats and the sparkly wrap went flying in various directions as the rack landed with a loud crash. Rubeo now lay stretched out across the hallway, totally startled at such an unexpected, jarring movement and fully aware of being badly scratched with a top piece broken. It seemed that one of the arms that had so carefully provided service now lay beside the rack on the floor. Rubeo wondered what could have caused such a change in the pleasant life energy that had left earlier.

Filled with tremendous anger, the once quiet and happy human stomped off to another part of the premises, leaving the hat rack in a fallen state of disarray. A strange sight indeed, being stretched out on the floor with the carefully wrapped sparkly material that had previously provided such uplifting energy to the rack, lying askew and spread across the hallway. Even with the lights still on, the sparkle had lost its vibrancy, and after a few moments passed, darkness returned. The angry, off-balance, fumbling human somehow managed to return and turn out the lights, all the while muttering to himself, '*Never again, never again.*'

The next day, now back to his quiet demeanour, the human merely stepped over the hat rack and headed out the door, only to return with a can of shiny, dark liquid that he proceeded to brush all over the rack once it was put back to an upright position. It seemed that he was determined to obliterate any reminders of the past. The human took extra care to cover the words with thick gobs of paint in order to fill in the carved markings. The top part of the rack was left until later as he attempted to glue the top piece back together, tying the arm with a fine cord until the sticky glue hardened. The hat rack found itself plunked back in the corner, partially covered in glossy black paint. During the whole procedure, there was an odd sensation of life energy receding deep into the rack's core energy. Rubeo explained there was a strong urge to find solace from the covering of beautiful grain, which was no longer visible or free to breathe.

Time passed, and the human returned to check the rack and properly repair the damage. Once the rack was completely covered, he applied another layer of paint, and a few days later yet another that sealed any chance of energy escaping. A strange kind of silence took hold of Rubeo with the loss of warmth and vibrancy of exposed red cedar grain so deeply hidden behind this new appearance. The transformation was now complete. Resigned to the undeniable truth that life energy, weak as it was, would remain forever blocked, Rubeo the hat rack went into a deep, troubled sleep.

There was little to explain about the remaining time spent in such a dark, gloomy space being left with nothing to measure any seasonal time passing. Sadly for the rack, with no real awareness of movement, light, or sounds other than a very faint energy vibration whenever the Quiet One quickly passed, all awareness of cedar life energy would forever stay in a dark living tomb. The rack remained in this comatose state up until a thin opening of light shone into the darkness, spurred on from an extraordinary moment of awareness that took place with the life energy of the Quiet One at a much later time.

Although a great deal of time had passed, long after the dreadful scene with such a profound gloomy result, Rubeo was soon to be reunited with Cedrina, in the home of the Dear Ones. However, before being rejoined, a most peculiar event took place in that dark and dreary passageway, bringing a glimmer of hope for the rack. It turned out to be the very last time of awareness contact with the anxious human, who until that moment rarely came into the hallway. Approaching the rack with any kind of contact was something the

Quiet One had not attempted since transforming it into the cool, shiny pole it now represented.

During this most peculiar event in the life energy of the cedar hat rack, the quiet human came into the hallway and slowly slid down the wall, coming to a sitting position close to Rubeo. The energy being released was so deep that in spite of the layers of paint, Rubeo was able to detect a very heart-rending energy vibration from the human. It seemed at this point, he was filled with regret for his actions and treatment of this precious gift, and as the remorseful human again reached out in apology his kind hands gently caressed the area on the pole where the old scar had previously been visible. This action brought great relief into the dark tomb in which Rubeo was trapped, and it provided intuitive awareness to the rack that there was indeed a light at the end of the dreariness that surrounded its cedar energy.

It was while slowly moving his hands along the base block of the rack, where the carving lay hidden, that the Quiet One repeated these words many times over. *'I am sorry. Please forgive me. Thank you, for the precious gift of love. I love you.'* The hat rack knew that the words were spoken with deep remorse, and that they were meant for the Dear One, who was not available at the time to hear them. Intuitively, Rubeo knew a time would arrive when the Dear One would receive this deep, heartfelt energy message as intended. It was the last remembrance the hat rack held of this troubled human, and he was uncertain how much time had slipped by before being reunited with Cedrina once again on a very cold winter's day in the peaceful alcove nestled in the home of the Dear Ones.

Although the rack could not connect with Cedrina in those early alcove days, the deep, dreary darkness that overshadowed its energy slowly dissipated. Rubeo had returned to a place of belonging, and over time began to again sense deep contentment within the quiet solitude of the alcove atmosphere.

After sharing the missing pieces of the cedar story with the alcove companions, Rubeo was now completely at rest as never before. It had been such a relief, in this magical moment of blue, that a precious gift of expression had enabled the story to come out, along with awareness of the heartfelt quest for forgiveness from the Anxious One of the past. The little cedar story has almost come full circle with the sharing of the hat rack's life energy connection with the Quiet One. There was an interest to what actually took place in the life of one so troubled. Perhaps before leaving these peaceful surroundings in the next few days, the Anxious One's full story would indeed be revealed.

FILLING IN THE BLANKS

The guest understood that Rubeo 's, Quiet One was a very close friend to Cedrina's Dear One, and she was determined to find a way to pass on the awareness of what Rubeo had related as a request for forgiveness. The story of this troubled human was made known to the guest sometime ago, and for the most part she was able to follow his life story.

It seemed that the anxiety-riddled human had in adulthood lived a hard life, suffering greatly from the effects from strong drink that did not bode well for him. Past memories filled with regrets over life decisions made when he was a young man kept him in a tight grip of emotional pain. Overcoming this remorse and ensuing hardships for many of the poor choices he had made during a great deal of his adult life had taken its toll, making it difficult for him to find any real happiness. It was just after the longest period of peace and comfort, which finally came much later in life, that a difficult health situation, emerged causing a temporary backslide into the abyss of a past destructive pattern. Although this condition was short-lived, it proved his undoing, and soon thereafter he passed on, hopefully to a place of peace. He was deserving of freedom from pain and suffering, especially because in his heart, he was actually a very gentle soul whose life energy had turned into such a tortured spirit while on this earth.

The early morning gift of blue provided the guest with much food for thought during those moments of connection, strengthened by the energetic purring of Furry Four Legs. It had been a surreal sharing opportunity, basking in a combination of vibration and colour and the combined energy of the companions; it was a truly magical catalyst to the remarkable stories that followed. One could only marvel at what a great relief it must be for Rubeo, finally able to connect and express separation experiences that could only add strength to the intertwining of the two red cedar energies now able to combine as one. This strong connecting ability brought resolve to the original cedar tree desire to be of service to humans in spite of all the hardships the pair had endured. Oddly enough, it was the very nature of the separation experience that had such a profound influence on finding peace for the dear friend of the creator of the cedar duo. In the end, the entwined cedar energy achieved meaningful purpose on many levels.

Uplifting words came to the surface for the guest. These particular words spoke not only for all that had played a part in the cedar's separation story, but also to any of life energies that could relate to a need for finding love and appreciation during hardships from many of life's experiences. *'I choose to allow all my experiences to be filled with loving gratitude. It is with flexibility and ease that I choose to see and express all sides of an issue. I am safe.'*

Moment of Reflection

Blue: 'Throat Chakra focuses Communication/Creativity/ Sound/Intuition/Self expression/Desire to speak and hear the truth' (<u>www.expressionsofspirit.com</u>).

To Speak

An interesting aspect of self-expression and communication expressed by the anxious human to Rubeo during their last connection experience closely resembles the ancient practice of a Ho'oponopono prayer (http://reikirays.com/14628/ ho'oponopono/). It is understood by those who practice this prayer, when spoken from the heart, that the great power of forgiving energy is possible for both the giver and receiver.

Could it be that a healing of sorts actually comes through, unburdening one by means of repeating these words?

Perhaps it really is possible for an enlightening shift in life energy to take place for those who are able to find expression and make use of such a meaningful prayer.

ENERGY GIFT OF INSIGHT – TO SEE

Predawn arrived as the darkened room slowly opened to daylight, chasing away lingering remnants of deep night-time hidden shadows. It took but a moment for a spectacular, brilliant colour display of indigo to come streaming through the glass water prism. To the alcove companions, it was like opening a magical door of enchantment and becoming immersed in a deep glow of inspirational energy slowly cascading over and through each member of the little group. While absorbing this magnificent energy experience, each was left with a sense of having been thoroughly cleansed from any lingering shadows of doubt or fears that had been hidden deep within them.

By now accustomed to the early morning light display, Cedrina and her alcove companions continued to marvel at the smoothness of connection taking place. In this moment, it seemed that once more the group's individual energies effortlessly entwined into an awe-inspiring sense of oneness. This energy gift of colour was no exception to past tranquil colourful moments shared, and each of the companions could not help but find comfort in its force. Quiet contemplation took root in the peaceful atmosphere of intriguing indigo, which stimulated for each of the companions a powerful experience of being fully aware and awake in the middle of a dream world.

Although very complex, this most unusual experience could only be described as a heart and mind awareness that slowly blossomed to a point of focusing on three things at the same time. The sensation was likened to that of having complete awareness as a group energy bound together, finding themselves surrounded by a spiralling whirlpool of energy. At the same time, each in the group was very aware of an unusual motion being created by the light actually twirling around and through them at the same time. It was very difficult for the group to put this truly magical experience to words. How was it that four individuals could actually be in the very same centre space as one, and at the exact same time be caught up as separate individuals in a swirling space? During this experience each companion could perceive what was about to take place.

Not surprisingly, each witnessed the room filling up with small, multicoloured globes of energy, vibrating at different rates as they magically materialized from different directions. A compelling sense of fascination accompanied each of the individual globes. The little group knew what was about to take place as they observed each of the floating globes slowly gathering close together to form a tight cluster. Then, as if the companions were willing it to happen, the cluster began to slow down, and in some cases speed up, until all individual vibrations were pulsating in unison. Amazingly, this animated cluster effortlessly turned into a single, multicoloured, highly charged, powerful ball of energy before bursting outward, sending minuscule colours throughout the little alcove space. Time stood still for this little group, and there was no way of determining how long this extraordinary vision experience lasted. Surprisingly, as the deep indigo light dissipated, what remained was the strong, surreal bond of being part of one entity or sense of oneness.

The group was captivated by this experience, and it took a few moments before focus was brought back to the room. The guest once again took pen in hand and began writing about the unusual experience. She gave consideration to an affirmation that came to mind during the initial purring from Furry Four Legs, just before the enthralling experience began. *'From deep within, where lies an infinite well of love and appreciation, the life energies of all in this moment can joyously move forward, embracing what comes from this magical connection.'* How fitting that these words were in direct correlation with what had taken place during the powerful moments of colour energy. The guest pondered on a past understanding regarding the name 'Ajna' given to the indigo brow chakra, which means both to perceive and to command.

Considering the meaning of what had just transpired, there was an instant alertness for the guest, very much like turning on a light switch, that triggered an '*Ah, I see*' moment in relation to the strength of connection that took place between the four companions. How odd that understanding something so profound in heart and mind, was not easily transferrable to writing. However, in this case she was determined to give it a go. What follows is based on her expanded understanding to a creative-force moment of awareness that had arrived at the same time to each of the companions experiencing this unique indigo gift.

From Furry Four Legs came awareness that translated as, '*This is the place where life energy guided me to be, a place where I would love and be loved, heal and be healed, and contribute to others beyond my previous simple survival instinct.*' Based on what was understood with the inspiring story of the tiny fur ball's arrival at this household and the events that followed, the words seemed very appropriate. They were not all that surprising coming from the dear tiny creature, because there was much magic and mystery about Furry Four Legs. The guest was sure that there was much more than met the eye to this tiny creature, and only time could reveal its depth.

What the guest understood from Cedrina and Rubeo, being two separate energy forms stemming from a single awareness surfaced, and that translated into the following declaration. '*We have come full circle from a place of belonging residing as one, moving forward to a place of separation, only to be reunited to a new place of belonging, still separate in form and now once more able to reconnect as one. We have followed an unusual path that put us in the right place at the right time, and we rejoice in what was, what now is, and what is yet to come.'* How appropriate were the words that described what had taken place in the life energy of Rubeo Cedrina, little red cedar.

The energies were truly separate, yet at the same time they remained as one cedar energy. The guest felt a very strong desire to allow the future to unfold day by day and moment by moment. What had taken place with Rubeo and Cedrina proved miraculous to the guest. There would need to be a larger-than-life energy force at work, paving the way to experience these magnificent moments of sharing stories and insights that came together in such an unusual way. It was hoped that this awareness connection would continue wherever and whenever the foursome gathered together.

On reflecting about her own past, the guest became aware of the times when life did not work out as planned. Her past contained many moments, days, and even years filled with challenges that led to unexpected outcomes, not exactly fitting with her dreams, hopes, wants, or desires. With this in mind, the guest recalled a favourite quote she often used as a personal mantra that had a profound effect on her thoughts, influencing personal life choices in the past.

'If one advances confidently in the direction
of his dreams, and endeavours to live the life

*which he has imagined, he will meet with a
success unexpected in common hours.'*

—*Henry David Thoreau*

In hindsight, she could easily see where a lack of trust in following one's own intuition came into play. There had been many times in the past where two specific, clear choices were presented to her conscious mind. Both choices were thoroughly questioned before a choice was made or direction was taken. For the most part, due to a lack of trusting the unknowns of the future, the inevitable choice was highly influenced by taking the well-understood path.

Unfortunately, the guest found that in taking a path of least resistance often resulted in unsatisfactory outcomes. Following this pattern of making choices created increasing frustration with what had previously been understood or desired as her true life path. The *'Ah, I see'* moment came with the realization that when faced with challenges throughout life requiring important decisions, it is more important to listen and act on deep, inner 'gut feelings', which she now understood, would bring more fulfilling conclusions. She had found that this type of gut feeling listening, understood as 'intuitive awareness,' was so much more reliable when making life-altering choices.

Another way of putting it, for the guest, was the understanding that when choosing from a place of intuitiveness, there was less chance of becoming stuck in a quandary of instant and often superficial emotion. The emotions in question would be made up of fear, anger, and frustration, or even sometimes sadness – all primary responses to challenging situations. As she looked back, it became apparent to the guest that those very emotional, quick responses to situations had actually undermined the intended outcomes of past life choices. You could say that many of our life choices outcomes are not all that different than those of the Anxious One; once having made the choice, you must live out the outcome no matter how unsettling it was to one's own psyche. How extraordinary it was to find that over time, one could see how past decisions actually fit with present life circumstances. One could wonder, does it really matter if so many life goals are made from dreams and achievements based on hopes and desires of the past? How strange that at the time they seemed so very important to her happiness.

The guest had answered the call to come to this place at this time based on intuitive awareness, unknowingly leading to a greater, higher purpose of service, as well as the notion to be of help to her loved ones. There had been other issues that also called for her attention back home, and had they won out – well, simply thinking about what would have been missed if the choice to follow the familiar took priority over the gut feeling, which at this time was difficult to fathom.

Moment of Reflection

Indigo: 'Brow Chakra Knowingness/intuition/Perception, Self Mastery, wisdom, imagination' (www.expressionsofspirit.com).

To See

Life is in a constant flow of change, sometimes with little choice to be made due to many unavoidable, life-altering changes taking place. One could conclude that no matter the outcome, life's direction is also in a constant motion of change.

Perhaps living and learning from one's choices is the most important component of any experience; it actually plays a major role in the process of expanding one's mind, body, and spirit.

Could it be that trusting in one's own energy force by listening and developing a strong intuitive awareness will point the way towards a remarkable future filled with amazing experiences?

APPRECIATING PAST AND PRESENT

CHERISHING YESTERDAY

After experiencing the energy from the wonderful colour gift of indigo, Cedrina felt completely free of all doubts and uncertainty of the future changes that were about to take place. While pondering this new sensation, the little bench came to a greater appreciation of her past experiences and now considered them as gifts to be treasured. It seemed that as a cedar bench more acutely aware of her cedar past through dream memories from the lake area, it was more plausible to keep hold of appreciation for all life experiences. For the bench, the miracle of life was being able to experience a variety of awareness connections with other life-forms.

Cedrina had to admit that her past and present overflowed with exciting life adventures through many unusual and unique energy connections. She was truly astonished at all the possibilities that accompanied each of the experiences that took place or could have taken place, and that brought a new appreciation and awareness to her life cycle. Cedrina had come to understand that the natural order of experience for all species within a predictable life span could be easily interrupted by circumstances outside their own influence. This awareness was specifically tied to the scarring incident: so many possibilities emerged from that one incident that was in another's control. However, looking at what might have been if the incident had never took place left no comparison for the amazing outcome created by the incident. And so it seemed, at least for Cedrina, no matter what happened in a life energy cycle, finding contentment and purpose was completely tied to energy experiences and the ability to appreciate all possible outcomes.

Cedrina was now able to better appreciate all nuances that took place in both past and present, from her maturing cycles in forest life surroundings. Her appreciation turned to the ongoing changes through the unfathomable seasonal possibilities based merely on a natural order of the life energy of the pristine lake, and how they brought not only pleasure and contentment, but magic and wonder to the surrounding forest life. This wonderful lake was the bearer of abundant gifts of life, and it overflowed with a profusion of pure joy for all who took advantage of what was available. Cedrina took in the comings and the goings of interaction with currents, the air, the sun, and the moon, all impacting the little lake and in turn impacting the life-forms influenced by what was offered through lake energy. The little lake was able to provide a place of refuge, nourishment, and unfathomable life energy for the water creatures, just as it offered a means of passage for humans with their boats that skimmed the surface as a means for travel and entertainment.

Dream-memories flooded back in flashes to the little bench, filling her with more appreciation for the natural beauty found during the various seasonal cycles of the forest lake found high in the mountains. A dream-memory whispered softly, with the wonderful panoramic views that slowly emerged during the changing seasons. There was a vision of the silent, frozen beauty of snow-filled wonder, with minimal energy movement other than the howling of cold winds trying to awaken life-forms found in the deep sleep of winter. It was as if the little lake itself had gone to sleep in spite of the slow-moving life energy that took place beneath the sheets of ice covering the water's surface. This icy view was followed by memory flashes of the sights and sounds of early spring and of small creatures found foraging for nourishment found under the melting snows. The atmosphere of silence came alive with the young cedar's awareness of newly awakened creatures, observed with all the hunting, playing, and mating antics that would take place in and around the lake.

There were distinct dream-memories of early evening as the bright light slowly dimmed, following its own journey cycle, leaving room for the calming solitude of the lesser light, and shimmering ripples over the smooth lake surface. This solitude was only broken with the gentle sounds of early and late evening creatures, replacing the higher activity sounds of life-forms that had settled for the night. The mighty storms that would sometimes come off of the lake from the gusty winds of fall, and the cold winds of winter, spread a powerful energy that could not be easily forgotten. How wonderful that these observations from the past, as memories for Cedrina, also took place with other trees in the present; the little lake continued providing life awareness with all its immeasurable energy possibilities and outcomes. Cedrina considered it a privilege to have been part of such a beautiful scenic space as a young tree.

Still feeling the joy from the early morning gift of indigo, Cedrina pondered on the abundant learning opportunities that stemmed from her tree life energy, which were now safely stored away as dream- memories and could be easily retrieved. Recollections of forest surroundings soon returned as Cedrina turned to her awareness from shared memory stories of driftwood life energy that washed ashore. They were like bits and pieces of nature that were going through a transformation of their own. Some of the information shared by these bits of nature's life-forms came about by premature ending circumstances, whereas others were tales from a natural life span ending. Amazingly, this occurrence in nature provided unique connection potential through direct contact with other curious life- forms, which could not resist investigating what had been washed ashore as a gift from the lake and hurried back to share what was learned with the little red cedar. It was this simple act of sharing that brought far-reaching stories from the extensive forest areas that surrounded the lake. Much was to be learned from the never-ending driftwood stories explaining countless possibilities of life experiences for her species as a tree.

The red cedar learned at a very early stage of development that the most important message gleaned from the awareness tales related to the joy and pleasure to be found in each and every adventure experience. Cedrina had learned that interesting and important learning came at a time when the time for sharing was fast coming to an end. It was extraordinary to find that each shared experience related the same message: contentment and sense of joy came with all facets of life experiences, and it lingered in whatever remained of life energy. There was always joy in the tales being shared, whether related to being cut down by humans to be used for strange and unusual purposes, or from a time when decomposing from age took place, or even from an early demise due to disease. Each tree life experience held intrinsic knowledge that could be found in all parts, and no matter the reason, life energy would continue in some form or another.

Cedrina also marvelled at the many driftwood stories, some of which related to having been ripped out by the roots during a violent storm. Others proclaimed that they had become rigid and hollow while being consumed by small creatures. Over time the hollowed trees were unable to bend with strong winds, snapping into pieces as they fell to the forest floor. Some of the fallen trees residing close to the shoreline would be swept up by the high tides of early spring and pulled out into the lake waters, to be carried away by strong currents. There were tales that brought great concern at having life energy disrupted by the experience of tremendous transitional change as a result of fire. In those cases, so much of their tree energy would be blown away as ash, leaving only small stumps and weakened roots to share the tale. It seemed to Cedrina that no matter the circumstances or size of the driftwood, there was genuine happiness to have ended up at this beautiful forest lake. Many driftwood portions explained to her that it was like floating through a magical door, coming to a final resting place, and having the chance to continue in purpose and service while still having some life energy to offer other life-forms.

Cedrina realised that her cedar tree parts that remained in the forest would stay to be absorbed into Mother Earth, enriching the soil. Some of her branches would be able to hold on to precious seeds and could later let them go to be reborn and start the cycle over again. It was satisfying to know that some of her tree life energy ending was not all that different from the other trees found in the surrounding forest. Cedrina would remain calm and serene, much like the little lake area where her life cycle began; staying confident that as a red cedar bench, she would continue holding pleasure and energy from dream whispers that would surface from time to time. For Cedrina, life could not get any better than that.

GRATITUDE WITH CHANGE

After being away for a few days, the Dear Ones returned with exciting news that all was going as planned. The property would soon be changing hands – and surprisingly enough, within the next few weeks. After closure day, they would be off to new life adventures. These dear humans would continue for a time, going through their own transitional phases of unique changes. This change lifestyle would provide the opportunity to retire gracefully in the peace and tranquillity that they both desired. Step by step, they would move forward, delighting in the upcoming journey filled with new and exciting life possibilities.

The Dear Ones declared to the little group that they were about to embark on a long-desired holiday trip before settling in for the summer at the lake property. At the end of the fall season, they would retire to the warmer climate area, staying with loved ones. Sharing this space with her Dear Ones had been quite an interesting life journey thus far, and Cedrina was happy for their joy and satisfaction of being able to fulfil lifelong dreams in retiring years. How advantageous to have been able to connect part of her Dear Ones' journey with the accomplishment of the cedar tree's past, filled with dreams of service to humans, especially as a young red cedar that had come through such incredible transition in the hands of loving human energy. There was much to be grateful for in servicing humans such as these Dear Ones, who in turn took such good care of the little cedar bench. They would be missed, and Cedrina hoped that before the next great change took place, there would be a few more precious moments of contact with the pair that played such a significant part in allowing her dreams of human service to come true. There certainly would always be room for a few more pleasant memories to store, keeping the memories alive in her cedar core energy.

Moments of Reflection

Many of us often consider what happens in life to be completely outside our control, and during those times finding happiness may prove difficult. However, it bodes well to remember that how we choose to react to what happens is completely in our control.

When we ponder the past, many significant experiences become heightened. As attention is drawn to them, it becomes very much like living them all over again. Our memory, or so it seems, can be likened to a two-edged sword.

One could find, when in the search for learning that comes from both happy and unhappy experiences, wisdom can be the outcome from any recollection. Recalling what was learned holds the power to bring much happiness.

DREAMING TOMORROW

Just as Cedrina wished, the very next morning, the Dear Ones arrived as they had in the past, with Furry Four Legs in hot pursuit. In spite of being a very bright, sunny morning in the little alcove, the event missed the magical light through prism presence, because the guest had taken the water container down to be cleaned and refilled. Still, the alcove atmosphere radiated peace, comfort, and love from the energy of these very precious humans. The extraordinary magic of the early morning's great light entrance would have to wait for another day.

A great sigh of contentment escaped from the Dear Ones as their furry pet curled up beside them and purred loudly. As if trying to speak to the space itself, the Dear Ones explained how much they would miss their special morning time spent in this peaceful place. It held great value for them as the perfect spot to re-energize, and they doubted that anything would ever be able to fill the gap, except perhaps the cookhouse with attached deck at the lake property – a definite possibility! So much had changed in their lives over the last little while, and of all the changes, the relaxing moments experienced in this space would inhabit their memories for a very long time. After the heartfelt thoughts were spoken out loud, a comfortable silence blossomed in the serenity of the peaceful atmosphere.

The precious moment of silence stretched out a bit longer as the Dear Ones sipped from their cups and longingly gazed out the window, quietly dreaming about their tomorrows. The silence was broken only by the arrival of the guest, who proceeded to hang up the little prism, now again full of sparkling water. It seemed to the bench that the prism felt joyful to be back, and it managed a twirl or two, sending sparkling rainbows in all directions. It was unable to provide an early sunrise spectacular gift of colour, because that precise magical light moment had past, but the glass container was still able to uplift spirits, bringing awareness to dreams of a bright tomorrow. The rainbow-coloured lights seemed to take turns landing on each of the life-forms enjoying the serene space.

Taking in this peaceful and soothing moment was made all the more special as the purring from Furry Four Legs increased in volume. The energy of the atmosphere provided the perfect setting for dreams of what the future would bring to all sharing the tranquillity of the moment. Not surprising, a delightful spirit of enchantment emerged as the life energy of each life-form in the room became immersed in feelings of love and appreciation for past memories, future adventures, and most of all the expansion of heart and mind that was currently taking place for them in this unique moment of connection!

No one could tell how long the enchantment lasted; each of the little group seemed far away in a distant dreamland, lost in a world where there was no measurement of time. This delightful spell held them captive until a faint musical sound, like a distant echo, called them back to the present. It turned out that the echo was no other than the chiming of a cuckoo clock on a shelf in the next room, waiting to be wrapped and packed away. No words were spoken about the spellbound experience; each secretly felt that putting the experience to words would break the enchantment.

After a few smiles and nods of mutual understanding for what had just happened, the Dear Ones broke the spell by discussing moving plans with the guest. It was explained that later this day, the new owners would arrive for a visit, to take room measurements and explore a bit more of the house and property. They also related that over the next few days, friends, family, and strangers would arrive to pick up various items from the outdoor sheds and from inside the house. Luckily, because all the items in the alcove now belonged to the guest, this little space would be spared the turmoil and sense of loss from the household purging that would be taking place. The last of what was to be kept would be loaded on a trailer at the end of this week, and a transport truck would arrive a few days later to pick up the trailer and take the possessions to a final destination. Fortunately, all would be leaving at the same time, and it would be on that final moving day that the little alcove furnishings would be carefully packed and loaded into a closed van, to begin a new journey that would start with a long trip to where the guest resided.

Absorbing this information, Cedrina realized that during these final preparations of moving and the high traffic soon to take place, the house would be filled with strange and unusual noises, not to mention unfamiliar energy vibrations from the comings and goings of strangers. There would be little time, if any, to experience new awareness connections. In fact, it would be surprising if anyone stopped long enough to enjoy the pleasant energy radiating from this special alcove. It could only be hoped that this unique space, where so much enchantment was shared, would be recognized as inspirational by the new owners as well.

All too soon, a cold, empty void took root – a substitute for the accustomed household sights and sounds. All Rubeo and Cedrina could do was witness the familiar warm energy slowly dissipate with all the packing and loading taking place. It was best to remember that this growing emptiness, similar to the transformation time in the past, would again result in a pleasant, phenomenal change. Based on past experience, life energy endings would be replaced with new, bright beginnings replacing the accustomed peace and tranquillity of familiar surroundings.

LATIN CARVING EXPLAINED

Later in the day, before breaking away from enjoying the last drop of dissipating relaxing energy, the guest found it an ideal time to ask about the words written on the backrest of the little cedar bench. Knowing that the bench was created from the hands of the Dear One, and knowing that Latin did not play any significant role in his life journey, her curiosity could no longer be contained. She expressed her query as something of interest, especially because the bench would become a part of a completely different household, and she felt it would be helpful to know the story behind the inscription.

The answer to her query did not come easy to the Dear One; his reason for adding the inscription was connected to someone who would remain very close to his heart. This deeply cared-for individual was of course, the Anxious One. He went on to explain when they both were young, the two were inseparable. They were best friends who grew up together and lived, laughed, and cried through many life adventures during the early days of youth. It was during the latter part of their schooling years as young men that they became separated. His dear friend went on a different path of education in the hopes of becoming a priest. The Dear One was very supportive with his friend's decision, and whenever they were able to get together for any length of time, he would offer assistance in the study of Latin, often quizzing his friend on pronunciation and meanings.

He then went on to explain why he had been being drawn to specific words relating to a statement of past, present, and future. These special words had been etched on a board in the old, dilapidated barn where they often hung out during their early years. The two friends would spend hours amusing themselves and making up scenarios of how these words could have appeared, sometimes coming up with outlandish tales of crazy possibilities. Unfortunately, the mystery of the etching on the barn board would never be solved; the builder had passed many generations ago.

The Dear One felt that there was a certain intriguing vibration and energy to the words, considering that the one who etched the words was more than likely a direct ancestor. As far as he was concerned, the words should be considered words of wisdom passed on as a message of great importance that would remain applicable to them both. It was during the education time in preparation for what was thought to be a calling for his dear friend that they decided to explore the Latin translation of the words that had become so important to them both. The words had become all the more important to the

Dear One since his friend had dropped out from his educational goal, becoming trapped in a quagmire of doubt. The Dear One believed that because of some difficult family experiences that played havoc with his friend, he was unable to let go of intense emotion and get on with his life. Unfortunately, this friend continued to feel that he was not good enough to follow the desires of his heart and mind. As the years progressed, the friend experienced a great deal of turmoil, and he regretted his decision to change his initial education goals and life calling.

When the Dear One was creating little bench, he decided to carve the Latin words as a reminder of a truly special time of connection to his friend, and to keep in mind the importance to those meaningful words. A most fascinating part of this story that took everyone by surprise was an explanation that the very same words, in English, carved in the base block of the hat rack were the very same carved on the barn board of so long ago. If the layers of paint were removed, they would be easily discovered. '*Cherish Yesterday – Dream Tomorrow – Live Today*' were now etched deep within heart and core of all who had the privilege of connecting with the story shared in this moment.

How appropriate that the two creations of the Dear One, meant to represent enchanting boyhood memories as a set, were divided between the two friends, only to be reunited as a set. Over the last few weeks, so much energy was spent in recalling past memories of the pair that pertained to the words in so many ways.

Those memories truly fit with the meaning behind 'Cherish Yesterday', and one could not forget what was about to take place as a reminder to them all to 'Dream Tomorrow'. There would be no hesitation in agreeing that 'Live Today' meant 'live in the moment' – exactly what had been taking place during the enjoyable experiences with the precious gifts of light and colour. And so it seemed that the whole household had been living the most valued words of wisdom coming from the past, to remind them to enjoy today and take full advantage living in joy with whatever the future brings.

An Unexpected Connection

It was late afternoon when the new owners arrived, eager to review what was needed to make the residence feel like home. The Dear Ones could barely contain their excitement as they met them at the front door. They were very pleased and astonished at the first words spoken by one of the new owners. '*Oh, my. Such a charming little space filled with welcoming vibes.*' The new owners had been so happy with the very first impression they had of the entrance way, and they asked outright if it was possible to buy both the bench and mirror. They thought that both items would fit perfectly with their own plans for this little space. The Dear One explained it was not possible, however if they were interested, there was another woodcrafted bench that he had made and stored in one of the sheds; it was similar in size, and although it was made of pine instead of cedar, he thought it would be a good fit for the space. The new owners agreed to have a look before they left.

Becoming aware of this new information for the first time, Cedrina wondered whether the bench in question came from the same forest lake area. She had recalled there were lots of pine trees that had been cut down during the clearing of the site. If so, the little bench could think of no better means of ensuring that a piece of the tranquility of the lake's energy would remain in this special alcove space even after they left. Not surprising, the pine bench was offered as a house-warming gesture, indicating that it would be a privilege to leave something of himself in gratitude for the many pleasant memories attached to this special place. This gesture was graciously accepted as a wonderful start for the new beginnings on which they were about to embark as they settled into these new surroundings.

The new owners were very pleased and appreciative of the property and all the special care that the Dear Ones had provided in its upkeep. They had been astonished at what had been accomplished; it was above and beyond the expectations in this general area. They felt the property was perfect for their family and their intentions to use the acreage as a horse farm. The fields and outbuildings were exactly what they had been searching for in order to house four riding horses. They were anxious to continue into the house and further explore other rooms. After calling out to their daughter to come in and see where she would like to have her room, they left the alcove space to begin the exploration of their new home.

Although there was no mention of discontent with their daughter having to move this far out into the country, it quickly became evident as soon as this young human came through the door. Cedrina immediately became aware of an agitated energy, and immediately named her the 'Reluctant One.' There was a great scowl on the young girls's face, so much so that it could be likened to a fast-forming thunder cloud, destined to cause much havoc on touchdown. The vibration of anger was quite noticable with every heavy step she took upon entry to the house. It was as if each step said, *'I don't want to be here.'* The Reluctant One did not even pause to take in the lovely view; she continued in her heavy-footed way into the interior of the house.

Cedrina, now able to pick up the vibrations of movement throughout the house, also sensed the increasing frustration felt by the new owners with the sulking, snarky remarks that came fast and furuous from their unenthusiastic daughter. Her response dampened the previous delight they'd felt as they continued from room to room. Within a very short time, the Relunctant One came stomping back into the alcove space and plunked herself down on the bench. Cedrina had no difficulty absorbing the high level of unhappy energy emitting from this human. The child sat with tighltly closed eyes as if to keep out any pleasing light that could possibly seep in and change such a determined cloudy dispostion. This unwavering gloom kept her in a dark, tighly locked space where no light was welcome.

Any glimmer of hope from the warm energy Cedrina emitted was rejected.

Before long, the young girl's rigid anger was slowly replaced with great sobs and tears of sorrow that flowed freely. These tears were considered a good sign, just like the lifting of a barrier to a fast-moving stream bursting to be freed. Cedrina hoped it was an important break that would loosen the strong grip of unhappiness keeping the young girl ensnared in her dark and dreary place. What was needed next was a spark of light that would touch her heart and mind, urging the tightly closed door to open enough to allow at least a sliver of healing light.

Right on time, answering the silent call, Furry Four Legs arrived, purring softly and taking a quiet stance beside the saddened human's feet. As if right on cue, as soon as the girls hand momentarily rested on the furry little head, the animal made a flying leap to her lap, followed by an increase of vibrant purring with each passing moment. Soon, Cedrina detected a crack in the armor of the Reluctant One's anger, and the previously closed door to heart and mind slowly opened. Intense healing energy penetrated the protected barriers to the girl's hardened heart, and without a moments notice, the guest came through the front door. In one fluid motion, the guest gave prism presence a twist as she walked by. Soon there were little rainbows of colour dancing about the space, reflecting off the mirror and adding to the magical healing effects from the ongoing purring that Furry Four Legs provided.

It took but a few moments for a simple smile to turn into delightful laughter at the magical light show and tremendous purring coming from the furry creature comfortably curled up on her lap. The purring volume and the young girl's delight was so high that it could be heard throughout the house, even in the lower area where the rest of the humans were busy exploring. Urged by the most delightful sounds, soon everyone was gathered at the doorway to witness the cosy sight, only to be totally surprised and facinated with what they heard.

Upon the arrival of her parents, the Reluctant One excalimed, *'What a wonderful little space. I am going to really enjoy spending time here.'* These words and what followed next warmed the hearts of all. The girl asked her parents if they would find a similar bench, a large mirror, and a water prism that could be a part of this delightful space once they took posession. The guest came over to the small human, placed her hand on her shoulder, and declared that the water prism would be left in the window to welcome her to her new home. Broad grins completed the return of harmony to the space, especially when the Dear One invited the young human to accompany her parents to view the promised handcrafted bench, the other house-warming gift.

Just when one thought it could not get any better, one of the Dear Ones came in with a tray of mugs filled with the rich aroma of her special brew. Each person received a steaming cup, providing the Dear Ones the opportunity to further explain the lure of the alcove space. It was with heartfelt glee that they enlightened the new owners of their own routine to come to this space and soak in early morning light while making plans for the day. It was wholeheartenly agreed by the new owners that this little alcove space would be a place of peace and harmony for them as well.

After the new owners left, the household once again settled into its normal, gentle, quiet energy. After returning to the alcove space, the guest was ready to journal the day's activity. The endearing experience of this day would surely stay with the new owners for quite some time, keeping with the alcove tradition as a special place of retreat. How marvellous it was that the items that were created with love and care by the Dear Ones would be also included. Of course, the handcrafted water prism's delightful contribution would add much pleasure to any new routines. It was gratifying to the guest that she was able to contribute loving energy that would continue long after she and the companions were gone.

Basking in this new awareness, knowing that it would be a combination of energies that would continue after they left, Cedrina quickly tuned into a forest lake memory. She was grateful that many small creatures would take advantage of the continuation of protection offered from the cedar energy that would come from the tree stub that remained. Leaving and giving off love and caring vibrational energy for others was indeed inspirational this day.

Moment of Reflection

It remains a mystery how healing energy can seep through the tiniest opening of a closed mind and, in such a small way, change the direction of negative emotion, allowing the heart and mind to open fuller to a happier state of being.

While basking in the magical pleasure of a water prism and reflected light, beauty with colour and light would capture anyone's imagination, moving heart and mind to one of appreciation and enjoyment.

Deep at the centre of all energy life-forms is an infinite well of energy where love resides; if received with joy and apprciation, light will enter. It then would be easy to conclule that light energy is a major conduit for healing energy.

Energy Gift of Understanding – To Know

A few days had passed since the unusual but inspiring visit from the new owners. Since then, many other humans had come and gone, never leaving empty-handed. There was a noticable shift in the natural energy about the house as items were taken away. It was a busy time for the Dear Ones and the guest, leaving little time to relax in the peaceful atmosphere of the alcove. It seemed it was the only room in the house that remained completely intact, and if anyone were to enter through the front entrance, it would look like nothing had changed. But changes were indeed taking place because everyone in the household was well aware that the normally warm atmosphere of the residence would never be the same again.

Furry Four Legs often hopped onto the bench for an afternoon nap, to get away from the upheaval that disrupted its favorite hiding places. There was too much activity and noise for this little furry creature, and so retreating to the one place that remained intact seemed the best bet. The most unusual vistor to the alcove during this hectic time was no other than Tessa, the pet dog. Finding a quiet corner in the alcove was the only reprieve from her tiring and noisy barking and no longer being able to get comfortable in her favorite spot in the kitchen corner. Tessa looked for the best place to rest her tired old bones, away from strangers and the household's hustle and bustle. The old pet quickly settled in for her usual afternoon nap at the same time as Furry Four Legs. At least they were able to find comfort in the only space that offered a reasonable amount of peace and quiet, and they settled for each other's company during such an fretful time.

The early morning light was going through a bit of a change as well. The position of sunrise was slowly making a seasonal change and, the previous glory and beauty of the first rays of daylight would be sorely missed. To add to this unstoppable dissapointment, heavy morning cloudcover appeared, and it was late afternoon before anyone was able to enjoy any warmth from sunshine. Cedrina wondered if there would be any more prism gifts of light; there were only a few mornings left before the final move would take place. There was the possiblity that the magic moments of colour previously experienced had run its course. It was thought by the companions it would more than likely be quite some time, if ever, before the magical show of light would return.

Both Rubeo and Cedrina were now emeshed in gloom, sensing a void over the change in the alcove's early morning routine. They hoped that there would be at least one more captivating connection before travel desended upon them. Eventually the hustle and bustle settled, and by early evening the Dear Ones had an opportunity to take a long-awaited break. A huge sigh of releif was heard when the last of the items in need of collecting left that afternoon. Both were looking forward to a much-deserved sleep-in during the next few mornings, before the final packing. Joining in the conversation during this hard-earned relaxing moment, the guest indicated that it would be heavenly to take in one more early morning sunrise, although the weather was calling for cloudy days up until the morning of their departure. Anticipation to a less hectic atmosphere was in the hearts of all that evening, looking forward to much calmer days ahead in order to complete the final preperations for the big move. A huge sigh of relief was heard from them all, including the dog.

True to form, during the next cloudless morning, the great light once again appeared. Just as before, it rose over the horizen and slowly creeped across the ground. This time as the early morning rays entered the alcove windows, the intensity of light was far different. As these rays hit prism presence, euphoria washed over every particle of life energy in the alcove space. The light slowly and gradually filled the room with a delightful, soft violet hue. The warmth of this colour energy expanded like a heavy mist, getting ready to turn into refreshing tiny drops of rain and bringing nourishment and life to a thirsty, arid space. As the light hit the mirror, the vibrant effects reflecting back gave the appearance of a bursting cloud sending out tiny beads of vilot throughout the alcove. Soaking up this astonishing show of light was much like being in a wonderful trance absorbing a deep violet haze. It was soon hard to tell where it began or where it ended, and it was difficult to discern whether one was surrounded by the mist – or whether one was the mist itself.

The power and intensity of energy from this spectacular gift was enthralling, so much so that it took a few moments before realising the quiet entrance of the guest carrying Furry Four Legs in her arms. The first recognition of arrival came with a vibrational awareness of deep compassion and profound love filtering through to Cedrina's cedar energy core as they gently sat on the padded surface of the bench. The light had caused such intensity in the little bench that it was enough to take one's breath away, and the guest let out a long, deep sigh while slowly taking in the powerful enchantment revealed through the water prism's breathtaking gift of violet.

Cedrina was coming to truly understand what she had known all along about sacredness, which in the past had remained partically hidden, seemingly mysterious, and elusive – and yet at the same time, familier and obvious. Like a veil being lifted for the first time, the companions became aware of a conscious connection to a divine, creative force. The light switch of awareness had flipped from a belief to a knowing in that moment while experiencing this precious sacred colour gift. The soft violet glow led them to fuller awareness of the energy force that flowed through all of life in its many forms. The companions came to an enlightening understanding that there was no beginning or end to life energy.

Cedrina had awareness of an interrupted natural life span as a tree that had resulted in a fragmented energy state in present form as a cedar bench, and like all life energy, she would eventually return once more to the source. She finally understood that this creative force of power was within all things and included the familiar, divine source of great light that brought life to all existing energies on Mother Earth. A deeper meaning to 'all being well in my world' ensued, and had it not been for this colour energy being experienced, the little group wondered whether this fuller understanding would have even been possible. This was a question that would be difficult or even impossible to answer. It no longer mattered what would or could have been; the life energy of them all would be forever changed after encountering such creative consciousness in a moment that was altogether removed from space, time and everyday life.

Having now experienced this awareness, the guest found it difficult to find words that could describe what had taken place. It was like stepping through a dream threshold to a divine realm of consciousness itself, or at the least, the closest one could come in physical form.

The guest now truly understood the meaning of this violet colour connected to the crown chakra – a place to discover one's universal identity. For the guest, it represented a true meaning of self-knowledge, holding the possibility of comprehending existence as a spark in the mind of creation. To have experienced this kind of awareness, at this time and in this space, was truly a miraculous moment.

Thoughts now turned to the beginning life journey of the little cedar, which was so similar to the human life experience of entering existence in a burst of energy, followed by unquenchable curiosity in the early years of growth that would compel the cedar to reach out to immediate surroundings and make new life connections. It was not so far removed from the human experience because they too were soon filled with curiosity of life regarding maturing and growth, stretching out further afield and beyond, and never completely satisfied until awareness of existence formed within one's life energy in the here and now. There were so many similarities, such as the desires to fulfil dreams of service, the need to conquer fears of the unknown, and the inevitable challenge of learning to trust in the life process. All were equal parts of the life journey!

Based on this view, the guest viewed life as a miraculous, exploratory journey encompassing all facets of surfacing emotions while connecting and interacting with fellow travellers. Life for her seemed to be made up of an ever–changing life path while learning to live in harmony with all that crossed her path, expanding her ability to recognize joy-filled connections. The guest found that the experience of joy was easily found while sharing in the uniqueness of all aspects of life that intermingle with a desire for variety, beauty, and creativity – all the things that kept life so interesting. There was no question that life could be challenging. Perhaps it was those very challenges that were the basis for the wonder that could be found throughout this life adventure. Fulfilment of life could be achieved from both expected and unexpected outcomes.

It had been a most unusual morning of enlightenment for the companions, and after experiencing the wonderful gift of violet, they were better able to accept whatever life would bring in the future. The little group trusted that all things would work out, fully aware that the days to follow were bound to be difficult. The magic moments experienced from the prism's gifts of colour and light would remain an important element of a deep feeling of joy for each of them. There now was a core belief and certainty for them all that every person, place, and thing on this planet was interconnected with the energy of love. What had been experienced in this tiny space was a connection to that special, creative energy. Having understood what had taken place in these past early mornings reaffirmed to the guest the necessity to express love and appreciation for having been privileged to be a part of the unusual energy experiences of this alcove space before leaving for home.

Moment of Reflection

Violet: 'Crown Chakra stimulates, Intelligence/Bliss of Divine Wisdom' (www.expressionsofspirit.com).

When trying to share learning from this gift of violet, the profoundness of the experience may be difficult to comprehend in its translation. Like most spiritual perceptions, unless it is experienced, it remains difficult to explain or understand let alone accept without question.

Perhaps the awareness and learning from a colour gift such as what has been explained throughout these pages may remain elusive. However, when looking into facets of one's past and present life with the eyes of appreciation, a sharing door opens, bringing one to a semblance of fulfilment.

When considering the amassed knowledge gathered from all matter of life energy experiences that are found throughout the world and returned in energy form to the creative force, could the mere living of life be the catalyst behind any deeply seeded and strong desire to share what has been learned on the journey?

LETTING GO

It was late afternoon before the Dear Ones returned to take a break from the last-minute packing. Hats and scarfs were gathered, leaving the hat rack looking bare and a bit forlorn. Rubeo, not new to this empty sensation, recalled being a young tree stripped of branches and becoming aware for the first time that its folage would no longer be able to fulfill cedar tree purpose as a place of santuary. Although not as traumatic as that past transformation, the items that found refuge in the arms of the hat rack were again being taken away. Rubeo was thankful that there need not be any alteration in form involved with the changes that took place this time around. A very faint vibrational sensation was all that remained from each of the items that had been so delicately placed on the hat rack, because each item carried portions of energy of the Dear Ones. This missing energy would leave a void in the harmonious relationship to which the hat rack had become accustomed. It had been this very necessary service to the humans that replaced the cedar tree nature purpose. The connection to these humans had been intense, from earlier as a young tree through transformation in form and the mystifying connection experience with the Anxious One. For the hat rack, these combined life energy experiences would remain as cherished, intertwined dream-memories.

It was strange how it all worked out, eventually being reunited with a missing portion of form and finding such contentment in this space by the very same humans responsible for the change in tree life energy form and purpose. Although feeling a little off balance with yet another change, Rubeo was not overly concerned, knowing that harmony of purpose would again be found just around the corner with a new beginning, a new adventure, and a new place. No matter where or what doorway needed to be entered, awareness of safety would follow along with the peace and serenity of its early life energy beginnings, which could again be revived.

Satisfied with another delightful opportunity, Cedrina once again connected with the Dear Ones as they took a break, finding rest on top of the bench. The ensuing conversation was most reassuring. She as a cedar bench and chest had brought so much enjoyment to these humans. They had been discussing how much they were going to miss this alcove space and the special cedar chest bench that had helped fill their days with pleasure and contentment over the years. Fabulous energy again filled the alcove atmosphere, which could only be described as a santuary filled with peace and tranquility.

How marvellous that Rubeo and Cedrina were responsible for such soothing energy brought from the forest lake property. The Dear Ones would miss the important service that Cedrina had provided as a special place to keep handmade treasures safe and secure, and that was especially reassuring to the little bench. The Dear Ones had valued the sanctuary for the items stored in the bench's chest, and they indicated that they would miss the wonderful cedar aroma each time a new item was added or taken out to be displayed. Given the cedar tree's history and the emotional ties with this paticular little bench, it was impossible to find a replacement.

The chest of Cedrina was once again opened, and as the lid was lifted, the enchanting aroma arose to meet two smiling faces, enjoying for the last time the enthralling frangrance of red cedar. With tear-filled eyes, they unfolded the contents of the chest one by one while reminiscing about the pleasures and stories behind the handiwork of each item. Then they neatly folded and carefully transferred the items into a box, to be taken away. Understanding there would be astonishment and a response of joy, Cedrina's Dear One decided to leave one of the articles as a surprise for the guest. Thrilled with the brilliance of the plan and leaving a portion of love that went into every stitch of the item, knowing full well it would be safe in the heart of the little bench, brought pleasure to the Dear One.

So much love and caring energy from the Dear Ones encircled the transforamton from tree to treasured stroage chest having gone to extra lenghts into creating it to be a lovely and purposeful cedar bench as well. They both had been so pleased that such a usuful creation had stemmed from what was once a cherished lake site tree, found in a special place where peace and serenity were highly treasured. Then there were the words so delicately carved in the backrest. The creator of this unique artefact knew that the profound life message and unique story would live on and hopefully become as meaningful to future generations, becuase the little bench would defenitely continue service well beyond the Dear Ones' own life journey.

They both felt a sense of satisfaction that lightened the load for letting their treasure go as a gift to the guest, knowing that it would be accepted with love and appreciation. It was truly a pleasure knowing that this little bench would continue to collect love energy in its new home. Contentment was felt by both, finding that letting go of the little cedar bench was not the uncomfortable chore that they had at first envisioned.

Furry Four Legs and the guest arrived just as the lid was shut. The Dear Ones proclaimed that all its contents were removed and packed up, and it was important to tape the chest to ensure no damage would take place during the long journey ahead. The guest retreated and soon returned with tape in hand, which the Dear One immediately accepted after delicately putting the top cusion inside the chest. The guest was pleased that the cusion was to be part of the precious cargo, and she again indicated gratitude to the Dear Ones for these lovely alcove gifts, which would be treasured in heart and mind for a very long time.

All three humans then turned to admire the outdoor scenery, tuning in to the chattering world of winged creatures busy collecting food to feed the new life that had magically appeared. The humans had been so busy with the moving preperations that they had missed the new life season that was taking place all around them. They wondered if these small creatures would miss them as much as they would be missed, realising that these delightful sounds would no longer greet them and bring delight to their mid–morning ritual. Being able to watch and hear these wonderful sounds of nature had provided much pleasure, and very soon it would be the new owners enjoying the sights and sounds of the enchanted garden world they had created in which the winged creatures thrived. Based on the excitement and caring energy felt during their visit, it was likely that some type of pleasureable nature watching routine would indeed take place.

Tomorrow would be the last day to pack up and load household items before the planned early start, so this moment was the last of their morning appreciation rituals. The time of discussion was over, and it was time now to be busy, because there was still work to be done. Each one from the little gathering knew the final moment had come to let go, as they moved forward to a new journey. With much reverence, the guest sent a connecting affirmation message to the bench, hat rack, Furry Four Legs, and the space. *'This day is filled with appreciation for what was, as we forever cherish yesterday and dream tomorrow for what will be. We'll never forget what is taking place in this here and now, as we live today. All truly is and will be well in our world.'*

Letting go of this place of santuary was a tad bit harder than anticipated. Three more times that day, the group of humans found themselves coming back into the alcove space. Each time they allowed a moment to breathe in peace and calmness on this hectic day. For the Dear Ones, a lifetime of memories with family and friends, toil and hardship, laughter and tears – all was part of what would now be considered the past once they pulled out of the driveway for the last time. For the guest, it was a place filled with wonderful memories of sharing time and energy with these loved ones, along with a time of enchantment that may never be repeated. The past, present, and future seemed to intertwine, creating a special, pleasurable atmosphere in the hearts and minds of the three. A hectic, adventureous day of travel was about to begin.

Moment of Reflection

In order to make room for the future, one must first let go of the past. In order to appreciate that which is to come, one must cherish what has been.

By going with the natural flow and purposeful rhythm of life, it seems one must seek out what brings love and appreciation for all that accompanies an ever-changing life journey.

To truly live is to live from moment to moment, to live in the here and now of life.

PARTING OF THE WAYS

THE HUNT IS ON

It was very early in the morning, just before the break of dawn, when the majority of belongings were loaded on the trucks. So far things were going smoothly, and the weather was cooperating, providing a wonderful day for travel. If all went as planned, the journey would begin before morning light turned to noonday sun. The humans were taking a short break in one of the rooms downstairs, and the guest was busy trying to locate Furry Four Legs, who, not altogether unexpectedly, vanished in all the excitement. There had been so much commotion disturbing the furry one's quiet alcove refuge that hiding away seemed the only solution for some peace and quiet. Loud purring could be heard throughout the house, seemingly coming from every direction at once.

The little bundle of fur provided a much-needed, calming dose of its own healing power, however for the guest, anxiety rose as finding the furry creature's hiding place proved difficult. The hat rack and mirror had been carefully wrapped and loaded in the van, leaving only the little cedar bench that still needed to be covered and tied with a thick blanket to keep it safe. The guest thought it better to leave the covering of the bench till after Furry Four Legs was found and put safely into a travelling cage. No real problems were anticipated in the search of the tiny ball of fur, however in the excitement and eagerness to get going early, frustration slowly got a grip in the thoughts of the guest. Being unable to find Furry Four Legs created some aggravation for the guest, and she was becoming frazzled in the hunt. This hide-and-seek game took precedence over her one last chance to enjoy a special alcove moment with the bench and the parting pleasure that would surely come from the fast-approaching, marvellous sunrise.

Unfortunately at this point, the sunrise plan was doomed and now regarded as mere wishful thinking. Everyone wanted to get rolling as soon as possible, and so it needed to take a back seat on the priority list. While focusing on finding her four-legged friend, a new thought flashed to the guest's mind. *There must be a special hiding spot in the basement close to an air vent that carried the purring throughout the house.* Considering the loud purring taking place, this new thought seemed a very reasonable deduction. It was an ideal time, when the house was fairly quiet, leaving a greater chance of capturing the skittish ball of fur. The guest was sure that the tiny creature would need to be calmed down with some soft stroking and murmured reassurance in combination with its own soothing, vibrational sounds. Heartfelt compassion replaced the feelings of frustration. Focus now turned to purpose in order to prepare Furry Four Legs for the loading procedure that was to soon follow.

PRISM PARTING GIFT

The great light was just about ready to make a majestic appearance to an almost empty and barren space. The little cedar bench had been left alone as the last items to be loaded. Cedrina was now located at a most peculiar angle in the middle of the room, as if she was the only token life-form energy available to welcome the penetrating rays of the great light for the very last time. It was a strange sight unlike any other before, and undoubtedly there never would be again. A truly magical event arose when those first light rays hit the water prism, sending a brilliant rainbow reflection much like a halo effect that covered the little bench. What a shame that others were not present to witness the most extraordinary spectacle taking place. Like a great wave of pure joy, a most peculiar sensation deep within washed over the bench as the rainbow danced over and around her life energy form.

The rays of light provided warmth and glorious energy, replacing the dank coolness of the room. The ensuing energy warmed every fibre of the bench, wrapping her with unbelievable energy of colour and light. There was, in the briefest moment for Cedrina, awareness of pure, unfathomable ecstasy due to the intertwining energy connection taking place between her and the magical prism reflection from the great light. This coming together moment created unusual movement of light and colour, much like a kaleidoscope where each outburst was distinct and unique, displaying all the rainbow colours of iridescent beauty. The red cedar bench found it to be truly out of this world.

The entire scene seemed stranger because just moments before, the atmosphere was a dim and bleak picture of loneliness, with the little bench alone in the middle of a stark room. If one were to enter at this very moment in time, what a surprise one would receive. One would have witnessed such a lively atmosphere of the mixing of energies dancing about the space, slowly dissipating into a warm glow of daylight. Then in a moment's time, the room once again gave the impression of a comfortable space of peace and tranquillity.

The guest arrived with Furry Four Legs in her arms and gently sat on the bench to soak up some of the warm sunshine presently pouring through the window as a spotlight on the bench. Right on cue, the furry creature started to softly purr, and like a background chorus, the winged creatures outside sang joyful tunes that, at least to those present, relayed a farewell serenade. While sitting quietly in this very pleasant and momentarily peaceful atmosphere, the guest was able to reflect on the treasured moments that had been shared in this space.

The guest again became lost in the enchantment of a soothing connection. It was difficult to tell where the conclusions came from and whether they were from the guest or the little cedar bench or even Furry Four Legs; when one really thought about it, it did not matter. All that *did* matter was the surfacing of awareness to self and the creative force that stemmed from the life energies in that little room at that particular moment of time. Thoughtful words began to pour from her heart and mind. '*I am not the creator of myself. I am a small part of something much greater, and I'm aware that the greater part of me knows and completely understands the smaller me. I am a spark of a divine, creative force and am able to live according to my light energy and inward awareness. Although my vibration may change from time to time, my energy will remain, as will my dream-memories. I live out my existence in a constant state of change from one form to another, from one place to another, and from one attachment to another.*

'*I look back, but not with sadness or regrets for what could have been or with thoughts of what should have been. I look back with joy and appreciation for what was, and I'm very much aware that deep within my core, all that has taken place brought me to this point. All that surrounds me plays a profound and significant role in the beautiful energy that is me. I am becoming more aware of awakening spirit with expansion that can only come from transformation. It is how I view life's potential that stems from both positive and negative experiences encountered in the journey. My experiences have a great impact on my ability to withdraw or reject, to accept and adapt, or to simply go with the flow.*'

'We, this little group of companions, have come to a mutual conclusion that has served us well during this tale of enchantment. Embrace what comes, but take the time to love and learn from all that has transpired. Living in joy and harmony requires an attitude of gratitude for all that life brings through all life energy connections. As we embark on yet another change, we open both hearts and minds to all that will transpire in the future. We have come from a place of curiosity to belief, to knowing. Whatever comes will be filled with love and wonderful opportunities for joyful expression. All is truly well in our world! **'Heri Foveat – Cras Somnnia – Vivere Hadie'**

'Cherish Yesterday – Dream Tomorrow – Live Today'

Moment of Reflection

*In the end, it's not going to matter how many breaths you took, but how many **moments** that took your breath away.*

Shing Xiong

Life. Can it really be a spiritual sojourn, a physical endurance test, an adventure, or perhaps merely an opportunity to expand body, mind, and spirit?

It surely seems that the most significant factor of understanding comes with discovering love and appreciation for what crosses a life path during daily living. Each new connection is a unique possibility to expand awareness, offering new insight much like a sacred journey filled with miraculous bursts of love, energy, and bliss.

How astonishing it is that in a here and now moment of awareness, a sacred gift of connection arrived from an unusual energy life-form — that of a young red cedar tree.

What pleasure it has been, to offer a chance for Rubeo and Cedrina (little red cedar) to make a difference by telling their story.

Conclusion

And so, dear readers, it seems a remnant of the living energy of a great cedar tree continues, as witnessed by the incredible experience and deep appreciation for vibrational connections between all existing energy in this extraordinary world we call earth. I hope that the unique life insights found and expressed throughout this whimsical tale of connection will resonate just as meaningfully for you.

> *I am filled with love for all that was, all that is, and all that is yet to come. I awake to joy and peace as I love and live life with heart-centred intention.*
>
> Carolynn McCully

REFERENCES AND SUGGESTED READING

Tyler Vanderlyke. 'Cat Purrs Harness Holistic Healing Powers'. http://thespiritscience.net/2014/05/07/cat-purrs-harness-holistic-healing-powers/

The Fauna Communications Research Institute. http://www.animalvoice.com/catpurrP.htm.

Hilary Stewart. *Cedar: Tree of Life to the Northwest Coast Indians. D & M Publishers, Dec 1, 2009 (amazon.ca)*

David Pond. *Chakras for Beginners.* Liewellyn Publications, 1999.

Anodea Judith. *Eastern Body, Western Mind.* Celestial Arts Publishing, 1996.

Louise L. Hay. *You Can Heal Your Life.* Santa Monica: Hay House, 1984.

Sydney Banks. 'The Spiritual Nature of the Three Principles'. https://www.sydneybanks.org

Allan Flood. 'The Three Principles and Physical, Emotional and Spiritual Healing'. From *Awakening Experience*. https://www.**youtube**.com/watch?v= csAjZ1MwhPE

Printed in the United States
By Bookmasters